You Got This! 2

More Mental Game Skills for Young Softball Players

Dr. Curt Ickes

You Got This! 2

More Mental Game Skills for Young Softball Players

Portions of this book were previously published in *You Got This!* (2022) and *Win the Next Pitch* (2022).

First Paperback Edition: 2023 Published by KDP

Edited by: Olivia Fisher, Cynthia Hilston

Cover Illustrator: Hedri Widarmawan

Interior Illustrations: Jeanne Loiness(Vy Bui)

More Mental Game Skills
for Young Softball Players

Ava, Zoe, and the rest of the Southport Sting are back as they learn <u>more</u> mental game skills and set a new goal: to win championship rings in their first tournament of the season. There is just one problem: their old rivals, the Bandits, stand in their way.

Coach Moore announces to the Sting that they will attend a softball clinic at Coastal University where they will learn new mental game skills and play in their first tournament of the year. Zoe is ready! So far, the skills she's learned have made her a much better player. Can Zoe and the rest of the Sting apply these mental game skills to finally defeat the Bandits?

You Got This! 2: More Mental Game Skills for Young Softball Players, is the second book in a series that teaches important mental game skills to young softball players. These books are unique because sport psychology skills are typically taught at the high school, college, and professional levels. I've discovered that if these skills are taught in a fun and easy-to-understand manner, younger players can quickly make them part of their game.

The first book, *You Got This! Mental Game Skills for Young Softball Players,* introduces young players to basic mental game skills such as proper deep breathing to help control anxiety, the Three Ts of resetting after a mistake, and a proven four-step pre-pitch routine to maximize concentration at the plate. *It is strongly recommended that young players read book one before reading book two.*

In this book, readers will learn:

- **The importance of practicing the concepts from book one**
- **Adversity and failure are part of the game, so it's important to have a plan to overcome these situations**
- **To focus on things they can control, like emotions and attitude, rather than things they can't, such as umpires, weather, the crowd, etc.**
- **The importance of an Arrows-Out attitude rather than Arrows-In**

- What self-talk is and four rules of self-talk to help them play with confidence
- Ways to practice the mental game off the field so that these skills come naturally during a game

Coaches and parents: This book has a strategy guide that will walk you through the book as you teach these skills to young readers. This guide includes valuable suggestions on how to get the most out of each chapter, as well as specific activities to reinforce key concepts. A fun review section for players is also included.

This book isn't just about playing softball. The mental game skills that young readers will learn are also applicable to life off the field. They will learn how to deal with stress, develop positive self-talk, and create a plan for overcoming challenging situations. These abilities will help them in school, at home, and in any other stressful situation they may face.

Enjoy the book, and remember, *"You Got This!"*

Let's Go, Sting!

Table of Contents

1

Cookies, a Cat,
and Championship Dreams!

"Ouch! That looks like it hurts!" Ava scrunched her face as she studied the long scrape on Zoe's right arm.

The girls huddled on Ava's living room couch. The soft whirl of the ceiling fan filled the room. It was the morning after the Southport Sting's big game, and despite the sopping heat, the two girls buzzed with excitement.

Zoe nodded, turning her arm to study the scratch. "It does, but it was worth it. That was some game last night with the Wilmington Wildcats, wasn't it?" Her face lit up with pride as she turned her arm so Ava could get a better view.

"Yeah! And your slide home was so exciting. Darting home from third on that wild pitch was a great way to end it. I wasn't sure if you'd make it," Ava said.

"Me neither! But luckily, we won another one. Got those Wilmington Wildcats 3-2 and we're still undefeated! Go, Sting!" Zoe said.

The girls giggled.

Zoe's face grew serious as she reached up and wound a finger around a strand of her brown hair. "We have to keep playing well, especially when we play the Bandits. They're really good."

"The Bandits?" Ava asked as she tossed her long blond braid over her shoulder.

"Yeah, we played them three times in tournaments last year, and they crushed us every time. I think the closest game was like 10-2. They weren't very good sports about it either. Before the game, they all sneered at us, whispered, and then started laughing. When they shook hands after beating us, they would make funny faces. Addie and I overheard a few of them bragging to some girls on another team about how badly they beat us."

"Ava! Zoe! Would you like some fresh-baked cookies?" Ava's mom called from the kitchen.

"Sure!" the girls answered.

"I'll go get them and grab us something to drink," Ava said as she hopped up and made her way to the kitchen.

As Ava disappeared around the corner, Zoe noticed a big cat slowly walking into the room.

"Hey, Oliver! How are you, buddy? Are you getting used to your new house?" Oliver confidently took his time making his way over to the couch where Zoe was sitting. "I'm so glad your family moved to Southport. You're so cute!" Zoe exclaimed as she reached down and scratched behind his ears.

Oliver leaned in, stretching his neck towards her hand, and purred loudly.

"I still can't get over your short tail. Look at this scrape on my arm. It hurts, but I'm sure not as much as when you hurt your tail."

He seemed to understand her concern and nudged her leg with his broad head.

Zoe looked up as Ava came back in the room with a plate of cookies and some drinks.

"You know what? I was just talking to Oliver and told him that I'm so glad you moved to Southport." Zoe stopped petting his head to grab a hot, gooey cookie from the plate.

Oliver meowed in protest.

"Moving was pretty scary, but I've made great friends like you, Addie, Sophia, and the rest of the team. Everyone has been so nice to me. My family likes it here, too. It's starting to really feel like home," Ava said with a smile.

"I'm glad," Zoe said as she caught a big crumb that fell from her mouth.

"I also want to thank you for your help with the mental game. What you taught me has really helped me play better. When I think back to my last at-bat of the game, there was so much pressure, but I didn't feel very nervous after I did my pre-pitch routine."

Zoe stood up, cookie in hand, and pretended to approach home plate. "The deep breath and the focal point helped me not think or hear anything. All I saw was the ball leaving the pitcher's hand and heading towards the plate, and I ripped it!" She took a slow-motion swing and grinned.

"You did rip it! You're a great student. Do you remember when I taught you the steps and we first practiced them in the batting cage? It was something new and felt kind of strange, but I told you it would work, and it did!" Ava said with the tone of a proud teacher.

Ava nodded and continued, "You took that deep breath, studied the focal point, and then looked right out at my release point. The more we practiced that day, the better you got at it. It's all about practicing it until it becomes automatic."

"You're right. You were patient and reminded me to do each step slowly. I took my time with deep breathing. I studied the small focal point on my bat until I wasn't thinking about anything. Once I wasn't thinking of anything, my eyes went right out to your release point. At that exact moment, I was just seeing the ball out of your hand and all the way into the plate. No thinking. Just see the ball and hit the ball."

"With practice, the pre-pitch routine gets easier and quicker, doesn't it?" Ava asked with her eyebrows raised.

"Yeah! It's become automatic now, and it's amazing!" Zoe said as she stood up and, again, feigned swinging at an imaginary pitch.

Oliver watched, his whiskers twitching with amusement. Ava giggled.

"I also noticed that your fielding had improved, too, after I showed you how to use the reset when you make an error. If players don't use a reset right away, they get frustrated, and one error leads to another and another. It's like one bad play or one bad at-bat just snowballs. When that happens, it makes it harder to focus on the most important pitch of the game, the very next one," Ava said.

"Yep! Resetting with the *Three Ts* really helps. When I miss a ball, I *take* a deep breath, *throw* away the mistake, and *tell* myself something positive. There's nothing you can do to change a past mistake. It's about getting ready to make a great play on the next one. I'm a lot more confident now," Zoe said as she plopped down and chose another cookie from the plate balanced on the cushion between them.

"And it shows. I know that Coach Moore noticed it, too. My parents even noticed." Ava's phone buzzed. "It's a text from Coach Moore," she said as she studied her screen.

"What's it say?" Zoe asked as she leaned toward her friend.

Ava's eyes widened. "She's asking me if I could help her teach the mental game to the rest of the team at practice tomorrow. She also mentioned that she has a surprise in store for us. I wonder what it is…" Ava paused, her eyes glancing up.

"Hmmm, I don't know what it could be. I'm sure it's something really good." Zoe's face brightened.

She swallowed the last bite of cookie. "I'm glad you're going to show the rest of the girls what you taught me. We need to keep getting better, and learning the mental game will help us. I bet Coach Moore will have us practice them, too. I can hardly wait! It's going to be a great season for the Southport Sting."

8

Just then, Oliver sneezed loudly and rose from the couch. The nub of his short tail flicked up and he leapt down and stalked from the room. He plopped himself down in a patch of sunlight that shone through the front door's small window.

Ava laughed. "Oliver never feels like he gets enough attention."

"Poor Oliver," Zoe said sheepishly.

2

The Sting Learn the Mental Game

The morning sun peered through the leaves of the trees and cast shadows across the infield as the Sting gathered for practice. Its rays glistened off the still dewy blades of grass. The excited squeals of children playing on the nearby swings filled the air. A lawnmower hummed in the distance mingling with the dull roar of traffic.

"How's your arm?" Ava asked as she saw Zoe unpacking her bat bag in the dugout.

It still hurts if it touches anything, but it's okay. I'm ready to go today. Are you ready for practice?"

"You bet! Here come Sophia and Addie," Ava said, nodding towards the gate.

The girls watched as Addie playfully hit Sophia's arm with her glove. Sophia smacked her back.

"Hey, girls! How's it going? "Ava asked as she pulled her hair into a ponytail.

"Everything is great! Today I get to hang out with the best softball team in town. Go, Sting!" Addie said as she hopped into the dugout. Her blue eyes glistened with excitement. "Did we take care of those Wildcats or what?"

Just then she saw Zoe's arm. "Oh, that looks painful. Let me see it. Ouch!" she said, her nose wrinkling as she carefully inspected the long, ragged scrape. Then, with a smile, she added, "That was some slide, though."

"It hurts, but I'll be okay. Did you know that Ava is going to help Coach teach us mental game skills today? She showed me how to reset after a mistake, how to breathe the right way to relax, and how to focus on the ball when I bat. She knows what she's talking about."

"Really? I totally noticed you had a different routine when you batted last game. You looked more relaxed and confident," Addie said.

"Yeah, I noticed it too," Sophia chimed in, her brown eyes gleaming.

"I was. I was so focused on winning the next pitch, which is the most important pitch in the game," Zoe stated confidently as she bent down like she was playing shortstop.

The rest of the Sting arrived one-by-one, and the dugout bubbled with enthusiastic players as news of Ava's mental game skills spread. Coach Moore came around the corner of the dugout with a bucket of balls and her equipment bag.

"Hey, girls! Great game the other day. Are you ready to get better today?"

"Yes!" the team cheered.

"Well, we're going to try something a little different today. We're going to start our practice by working on mental game skills. You might have noticed that both Ava and Zoe used these skills during our last game," Coach Moore said while her eyes surveyed the group.

"We were just talking about it before you came!" Sophia said as she twisted her dark, curly hair into a ponytail.

"Super. I asked Ava if she would help me show you some of the mental game skills, and then we'll practice the steps later today."

The girls smiled as Coach Moore placed the bucket and equipment on the ground and paced around the dugout.

"Softball is played one pitch at a time. This is the most important thing to remember. No matter what just happened, your main job as a player is to be one hundred percent ready for the next pitch. That next pitch is the pitch that matters." Coach Moore paused.

The Sting bobbed their heads in acknowledgement, and she continued. "It's hard sometimes because there are so many things in a game that can distract you. Making errors, umpires, falling behind in the game, the weather, the fans, and the other team are all distractions that get in the way of

14

playing your best. Having a great mental game helps you ignore those things so your only focus is on the next pitch. Win the next pitch. That's the goal."

"But it's hard to forget a mistake," Addie protested. Her face pinched in frustration.

"I know it is, but I'm going to teach you how," Coach Moore said confidently.

"The first thing we all must understand is that mistakes happen. Even professionals who make millions of dollars still miss grounders. They still strike out. They still walk batters. They are the best players in the world and still make mistakes. It's just part of the game. If they can't play perfectly, we can't. We may not like it, but mistakes are bound to happen. Because mistakes are going to happen, we need to have a plan to reset. Your reset gets you one hundred percent ready to win the next pitch."

The coach continued, "You can't be thinking about the last play when the next pitch is thrown. When something goes wrong with your computer or video game, you press the reset button. It starts the whole thing over, like brand new. A good reset button in softball has three steps, which I call the Three Ts.

15

Take a deep breath, throw away the mistake, and tell yourself something positive."

"Let's look at the first step, the deep breath. It's not just a deep breath, but a special kind of deep breath. One that makes your body feel really calm. Do you want to show us, Ava?"

"Sure," Ava said, standing up and stepping in front of the group.

"This type of breath is when you breathe in through your nose and fill your belly with air. Then, you blow it all out of your mouth slowly. It's like you're smelling the flowers and then blowing out your birthday candles."

Coach Moore nodded. "Can everyone stand up, and we'll practice this?"

In the dugout, the girls stood and spread out.

"Let's try three or four nice, slow breaths. Ready? Go," the coach said.

The sound of slow, deep breaths filled the Sting's dugout mingling with the warm breeze.

"How did that make you feel?" the coach asked.

"It works!" Addie cried. "I feel a lot calmer. I'm about to fall asleep!"

The girls burst out laughing.

"What's the next T?" Sophia asked.

"The next T in the reset is to throw away the mistake. If you're in the field, you can pick up some dirt or grass, squeeze it, and throw it down. The dirt is your mistake, and you're getting rid of it forever. Pitchers, you can do this, too, after you have thrown a few bad pitches and are feeling frustrated," coach said as Ava demonstrated throwing away the mistake to the team.

"The important thing is that when you throw it away, it stays in the trash. No digging through the trash to bring it back out. Who would want to do that?" Coach Moore had a wide smile on her face.

Ava shook her head. "There's no need to think about it again. It's over, so let it go."

Coach Moore said, "The last T is to tell yourself something positive. You want to rebuild your confidence, so tell yourself positive things. Say something like, 'I'm the best shortstop in the league.'

Nothing gets past me. You got this! Those kinds of statements get you confident and ready for the next pitch."

Coach Moore leaned down and pulled paper and pencils from her bag and passed them out to each player. "I want you to write down the good things you will say to yourself if you make a mistake. You're not going to have to share them with me or anyone else. These are just for you to think about."

Zoe brushed her hair aside. She thought for a moment before scribbling her words across the page.

'Tough break.' 'You'll get the next one.'

'Time to make one of your great plays.' 'You can do it!'

Ava knew exactly what she wanted to write.

'Shake it off.' 'Stay tough.'

'Nothing gets by me.'

'No problem.' 'Let's get back to work.'

When the girls finished, Coach Moore said, "I want you to fold your paper and put it in your bat bag. Take it home with you so you can reread it and practice talking to yourself in a positive way. You can add more positive statements at any time. This is a great way to stay confident."

"Now, let's practice the Three Ts," Coach Moore went on. "Everyone stand and spread out. Imagine you just missed a ball, and the play is over. Go over your Three Ts slowly, then get back into position as if it were the next pitch. Show me how you'll handle the reset."

Coach Moore watched as the Sting performed the drill. She had them repeat it several times before saying, "Wow, that looks great! I see the determination on your faces! It's important that we practice this reset during our practices, so it's automatic during the games.

Zoe looked around and noticed her teammates. Their eyes were focused, their eyebrows drawn together. They were ready to go.

Coach Moore said, "Okay, we learned how to calm down using a deep breath and how to reset after a mistake. Now, let's learn how to concentrate on the softball right before each pitch. During an at-bat, a batter can be distracted by so many things. Can anyone tell me what some of those are?"

"Well, I can get distracted by everything going on around me. Sometimes, I hear the other bench chanting, and I can also hear what all the fans are saying. I try not to listen, but it's like I can't help it. I'll look at the pitcher's face, and if she looks mean, I get more nervous. Sometimes when I'm up there, my legs will even shake," Sophia said, biting her lip.

"I get distracted by my thoughts!" Addie said, "When I bat, it's like my mind is racing. I try to tell myself so many things, like to only swing at strikes, don't let a good pitch go by, and don't make an out. It's like a thousand different things!" She grimaced. "There's so much going on inside my head, I can't concentrate on the pitch."

"Those things happen to most hitters, especially in big games. Hitting is hard, so we need to have complete focus on the softball coming out of the pitcher's hand. Nothing else matters. Any distraction makes it tougher to concentrate," the coach said as she took a batting stance.

I'm going to teach you how to turn off your thoughts and focus on the ball from the pitcher's hand all the way to the plate. It's called a pre-pitch routine, and it's something most players your age aren't taught. I guarantee you'll be a better hitter the better you get at doing this routine," Coach Moore stated with assurance.

Zoe looked at Ava and nodded.

As Coach Moore continued, the Sting players hung on every word.

"The pre-pitch routine has four steps. The first thing you do is look at your coach to see the plan. Next, and this is an important step, is to take a deep breath to relax. It's the same kind of breath we talked about before. In through your nose, down into your stomach, and out of your mouth. It really relaxes you. You do this before each pitch. We want our shoulders and arms to be relaxed, so we can hit the ball harder."

"I noticed Ava and Zoe doing that last game," Addie called out.

"I saw that, too," Sophia quickly added.

Ava and Zoe smiled as the coach continued. "Step three is to look at a small spot on your bat. It makes no difference what you choose but pick something small. Look at it like you've never seen it before. Really look at it. It's sort of like your eyes are a microscope, and you're studying the details. Ava, do you want to show the girls what you use as your focal point?"

"Sure," Ava said as she grabbed her bat, and the other girls crowded around her.

"See this scuff right here, up towards the top? That's what I focus on. When I'm looking at it, I pay attention to the small edges. I'm not saying anything to myself. I'm just studying it like I've never seen anything like it."

The girls craned their necks so they could focus their attention on Ava's bat.

"All right, girls, grab your bats, and let's pick out what you're going to use as your focal point," Coach Moore said.

Each Sting player scoured their bat and showed Coach Moore what they'd use.

"How about this big letter here?" Addie asked.

"Let's try something very small. The smaller, the better," the coach instructed.

"I got it! I'm going to use this scratch," Addie said, pointing to a silver scrape across the bat's white barrel.

"Perfect!" Coach Moore smiled proudly.

The girls chose their focal points one by one, and Coach Moore made sure each was small and distinct.

"Let's practice turning our thinking off. I'll tell you to go. I want you to take a deep breath and look at your focal point. Ready? Go!"

They repeated this exercise several times before the coach asked, "Were you thinking anything at all while you were doing this?"

"No," Sophia offered.

"What about you, Addie? Did your mind race?"

"Nope. Zero. Nothing," Addie replied, raising her eyebrows. "Amazing!"

"Exactly. Using the focal point stops your thinking and blocks out distractions," the coach said, pushing her hands out to the side.

"The fourth and final step is moving your eyes from the focal point, directly out to the pitcher's release point. Your eyes only go to one place, the pitcher's release point. This is the spot by the pitcher's hip where she will release the ball. Don't look anywhere else! This helps you see the softball as soon as it leaves her hand and helps you track it all the way to the plate."

"It works, too. I didn't think or hear anything when I batted last game. I did the steps and saw the ball the whole way!" Zoe said, beaming.

we're going to practice this a lot today, so you'll use it in games," Coach Moore said. She divided the girls into groups and sent them to separate batting cages to practice.

The Sting players took the coaching seriously and followed each step. The sounds of solid contact filled the air as hard-hit softballs ricocheted off their bats.

"Wow! This is great," Sophia said to Ava after coming out of the batting cage. "It was like I could see the ball all the way to my bat. I wasn't thinking of anything. I was just seeing it, and if it was a strike, wham!"

Ava smiled, saying, "You'll get better at it the more you practice the steps. Did you notice everyone else was ripping the ball?"

Sophia tilted her head toward the batting cage. "I did! Look at Addie batting in there. She's always been a worrywart, but she looks like a different hitter. So confident."

"She does. I'm sure it's going to help everyone," Ava replied before taking a slow practice swing.

Coach Moore called the group together, and the Sting made their way to her, their faces flushed but proud.

"Great job, girls. What did you think?" she asked with a smile.

"It's awesome! I really felt better. It was like all those racing thoughts were gone. I can't wait to use it in our games," Addie said.

"Well, I have a surprise for you," the coach said, grinning. "We've been invited to a softball clinic at Coastal University this weekend. A friend of mine, Sharon Green, is their softball college coach and is holding a private clinic for four teams from the area. We're one of them. There will be lessons on pitching, hitting, and fielding with Coach Green and some of her college players. Also, there will be a mental game training session."

"That'll be so fun!" Ava said as the girls whooped and threw their arms around each other. An eager buzz of chatter filled the air.

"On Sunday, there will be a single elimination tournament for the four teams. The winners will get championship rings," Coach Moore continued above he excitement.

"Yes, alright, let's go!" the girls shouted.

"Who else will be there?" Sophia asked as the noise finally died down.

"It will be us, the Sharks, the Wolves, and the Bandits," the coach said.

Silence swept over the team.

"Great, just great, the Bandits are going to be there. We have to deal with them and their attitudes," Zoe mumbled as she rolled her eyes and looked at Ava and Sophia.

"Just what I wanted to hear. They're good, and they know it." Sophia said, shaking her head.

"Maybe we can beat them," offered Ava. "This is a new season. We just have to play our best game and see what happens. My last coach always said, 'The best team doesn't always win. It's the team that plays the best that day that wins.'"

The girls listened as Ava spoke. Not only was she the best player on the team, but she had played for the

Smithfield Scrappers, who won the state championship last year.

"You're right! We'll give it our best shot. Don't worry about what the Bandits say or do; just focus on what we can do to play our best. Play one pitch at a time softball," Zoe said.

3

Oh, Those Bandits!

On Saturday morning, Zoe's mother drove her and Ava to Coastal University. Tree-lined streets with large stone and brick buildings greeted them as the car made its way onto the busy campus. College students with backpacks and smartphones crisscrossed the streets and sidewalks. Some hurried, while others chatted and laughed as they ambled along. At the end of one street, Zoe spotted it, the Coastal University Fieldhouse. It was a huge building with modern windows. A Coastal University banner, which hung above the doors, gently stirred in the wind. The parking lot bustled with activity as players from the Sharks, Wolves, Sting, and Bandits got out of cars and milled around excitedly.

As Zoe's mom looked for a parking space, she stopped to let a group of Shark players cross.

"Wow, there sure are a lot of people here," Zoe said as her mother navigated the busy parking lot.

"Okay, we'll get out here. Thanks for bringing us, Mom," Zoe said, scanning her surroundings and biting her lower lip.

"Yes, thanks, Mrs. Davis," Ava echoed as she slid across the seat and climbed out.

"You're welcome. Good luck, girls!"

Zoe's heart pounded and her hands were slick with sweat as she stepped out of the car. She fumbled picking up her bat bag from the trunk.

"I'm nervous."

"What do you mean?" Ava asked as she slung her yellow and black Sting bag over her shoulder.

"I've never been to a big college or a clinic like this before. This is all new, and there are lots of girls here, including the Bandits. There they are, right over there. They can be mean, you know."

"New things make me nervous, too, but it'll be alright. I promise. Remember how taking a deep breath helps you relax while playing softball? It works the same way if you're nervous about other things. Let's take a few slow, deep breaths before we go in there," Ava said as they stopped walking toward the doors.

"Okay, good idea," Zoe said as she slowly rubbed the back of her neck.

"Breathe in through your nose and fill up that stomach. Blow out all that stress through your mouth," Ava instructed.

Zoe and Ava took several slow, deep breaths. Their heart rates slowed, and their shoulders loosened.

"Whew, that feels better," Zoe said. "Thanks."

"No problem," Ava said as she pulled the big door open and waved Zoe inside. "Let's go have fun and learn stuff."

They saw Coach Moore, another coach, and the rest of the Sting gathered near the doorway.

"Hey, girls!" Coach Moore called out to them as they got closer.

Zoe and Ava joined their teammates, and Coach Moore gestured to the coach beside her. "This is Coach Sharon Green. She was a teammate of mine in college and is now the coach here at Coastal University. She and her players are hosting the clinic. You'll learn so much from them."

"Hi, Sting! It's wonderful to have you here today. When Coach Moore and I played together, we had a lot of fun and won a lot of games. She's told me about your fantastic start to the season. She also told me you have been working on the mental game and have learned about deep breathing, the Three Ts, and a great pre-pitch routine. That's exciting because those skills help everyone play better. Because the mental game is so important, we're going to have a special session on it today. Are you ready to go?"

"Yeah!" the girls shouted.

"Super, let's go!" Coach Green said as she motioned for the Sting players to follow her outside.

She beckoned the other three teams to join them on the march outside to the Coastal University softball field. Once the large group gathered on the field, Coach Green introduced herself as well as the college players helping with the clinic. They went over the day's schedule before Coach Green had the girls do some warm-up stretches and start throwing to each other.

Zoe and Addie grabbed a softball, as did Ava and Sophia. Zoe and Ava stood along the first baseline beside each other.

As they waited for Addie and Sophia to jog to their spots across from them, several Bandits walked by, and a girl with a blond ponytail said, "Ooh, look, the Sting." The other Bandits giggled.

Zoe looked at the girls and gave Ava, who was on her left, a quick glance. Her jaw tightened as a tinge of rage washed over her. Ava shook her head and frowned.

Addie's first throw was low and glanced off Zoe's mitt. The ball skipped towards the Bandit player next to her, only stopping after it bounced off the girl's foot.

You might want to open your glove the next time," the Bandit said with a smirk while half-heartedly kicking the ball in Zoe's direction.

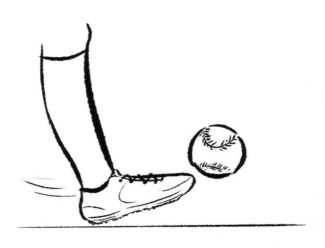

Zoe scooped up the ball and walked back to where Ava was standing and watching.

"What did she say to you?" she asked.

"Typical Bandit stuff. That's Chloe Wilson. She's obnoxious, and she isn't even the worst one," Zoe said before firing a strike to Addie.

"The tall brown-haired girl, number three over there, Kayla Pennington, is the real troublemaker." Zoe shot her eyes across the field and motioned with her head. "She's their pitcher and shortstop. She's also their star player and was really mouthy last year when they beat us. Kayla's the one Addie overheard talking badly about us after our game. I'd just stay away from her."

"Well, let's not worry about Kayla or the Bandits. Let's just focus on what we can do to get better today. Deal?" Ava said with a smile.

"Deal," Zoe said as she corralled another low throw from Addie on one hop.

After the girls warmed up, Coach Green divided them into groups. Zoe was glad that Ava and Addie were in her group but wasn't so happy about Kayla and several of the Bandits being part of it as well. Her eyes shot a quick glance at the Bandits walking their way. She turned to Addie and rolled her eyes in disgust. Ava had already headed towards the dugout for a quick drink.

Zoe grimaced as Kayla sauntered up to her. "What's up, Zoe? I see the Sting are back together this year. I look forward to playing against you girls again. I loved the batting practice we got in during last year's games," Kayla said with a grin.

Yeah, we got our exercise running around the bases, didn't we?" another Bandit girl chimed in and laughed.

"Who's the new girl?" Kayla pointed towards Ava, who was drinking from her water bottle.

"That's Ava. She just moved to Southport," Zoe said, bending down to retie her shoe and avoid Kayla's prying gaze.

"She's really good, too," Addie interjected, lifting her chin.

"And she decided to play with the Sting? Couldn't find anyone else to play for, huh?" Kayla laughed and nudged a Bandit player standing next to her. "You'd think that after last year, the Sting would have gotten like ten new players."

Addie winced as she remembered how badly the Bandits destroyed them last year.

"Funny. Real funny," Zoe said as her face heated. "C'mon, Addie, let's go take some grounders." Zoe smacked her mitt and ran to play shortstop.

Addie nodded and dashed to second base, trying to ignore what she just heard.

36

Kayla and the Bandit player trailed behind them to shortstop.

"I think I'll take a few grounders here, myself," she teased while her friend giggled behind her.

Zoe couldn't help but feel a renewed sense of determination. *We'll show Kayla and the Bandits this year!* She thought and readied herself for the first grounder, which she fielded cleanly and launched straight to first.

Addie didn't have as much luck. The first ball to her skidded off the turf and up her arm. She tracked the still-rolling ball down and tossed it to first. She shook her head and smacked her leg with her glove.

"Reset!" Zoe called out.

Addie nodded and walked behind the back of the line and did the Three Ts.

"What's up with that?" Kayla asked, with a taunting grin on her face.

Zoe ignored her question and snapped back, "Your turn."

The two girls watched as Addie made a great diving stop on the next hard ground ball her way.

"Nice play!" Coach Green yelled out at a smiling Addie.

"Great job, Addie! Way to reset!" Zoe called and gave a thumbs-up to the Sting second baseman.

"You think that was good? Watch this," Kayla said as she positioned herself for her ground ball.

When the coach hit an easy three hopper, Kayla tried to act cool and reach out with one hand. The ball skipped off her glove and rolled past her. Zoe looked at Addie and couldn't contain her giggle. Addie raised her eyebrows and grinned.

Kayla's eyebrows shot up, and she glanced around to see if anyone saw her misplay. The other players turned away as she caught them watching her. Kayla grunted in frustration and readied herself for the next ball. But ball after ball evaded her glove. It was almost like the softballs had eyes. With each error, Kayla's anger grew.

When yet another ground ball slipped past her, she pounded her glove on the turf. Kayla scowled as she stomped back to the end of the line, making sure not to look at Zoe.

Zoe and Addie glanced at each other, trying not to show their smirks.

"Reset," Addie called before turning and looking the other way.

After the fielding session, Zoe's group went to the batting cages for some hitting instruction. Zoe and Addie used their pre-pitch routines and ripped the ball. Kayla kept a close eye on both girls and said nothing.

When it was Kayla's turn to bat, Zoe and Addie could hear her muttering to herself about making so many mistakes on the field. Her teeth clenched, and she pounded the bat on home plate. When the first pitch came, Kayla took a huge swing.

Whoosh!

The bat flew through empty air.

She mumbled under her breath and smacked home plate with her bat once more, her face wrinkled with anger.

Again, a big swing and a miss. And then another, and another.

Pitch after pitch, she either missed the softball completely or tapped weak ground balls that barely made it past the pitcher. She became so frustrated that she swung at everything, including pitches in the dirt and pitches way over her head. Kayla was out of control.

"She needs a pre-pitch routine to calm down and refocus," Zoe murmured.

"Next!" the coach called, signaling a change in batters.

Kayla stomped out of the batting cage, yanked off her helmet, and slammed it to the ground. As she trudged over to get a drink, she didn't dare look at Zoe, Addie, or Ava.

"That's what happens when you don't use a good pre-pitch routine," Ava said to Zoe and Addie. "One bad swing led to another and then another. Did you see how mad she was at the end? There was no way she could concentrate on the pitch. That isn't playing one-pitch-at-a-time softball."

"I'm glad you and Coach Moore taught us how to use the pre-pitch routine," Addie said, and she slowly swung her bat.

When all the fielding, pitching, and hitting groups had finished, Coach Green called the groups together.

4

Arrows-Out All the Time

"All right, girls!" Coach Green shouted. "Let's take a quick break. Get yourself a drink, and we'll go into the classroom to learn about the mental game. I'll teach you what I teach the college team."

The girls hustled off the field towards a line of bat bags strewn next to the wall.

"This is going to be good," Zoe said as she stowed her bat and reached for her water bottle.

"I think so, too. We know some things, but there's a lot more to learn," Ava replied, wiping sweat from her brow.

Kayla and two other Bandits were standing nearby, and Ava couldn't help but overhear their conversation. "I don't care about any mental game training. We already destroy everyone we play, so why waste our time? I just need to get back in the batting cage and hit. That's more fun. Do you think they'd notice if we skipped this part?" she said with a laugh.

"Yeah, they would. I saw our coach by the classroom door looking around to see who was going in, so we'd better just go. We can sit in the back and do something like play on our phones. I'm sure it'll be boring," said one of the Bandits, rolling her eyes.

Kayla and the Bandits joined all the girls from the other three teams as they made their way into the classroom. The room was filled with tables, with an aisle running down the center. On each table were stapled packets with "Getting a Great Mental Game" across the top, along with colored pencils and markers.

Ava and Zoe took a seat in the back, across the aisle from Kayla and some of the Bandit players. Zoe noticed they were giggling and making faces at each other. One girl was already sending text messages on her phone.

"We're going to talk about mental game skills that will help you play better softball," Coach Green said as she approached the front. "Make sure you have the packet, pencils, and markers."

The coach wrote a question in big blue letters on the whiteboard and then read it to the young players.

"How much of the game of softball is mental?"

Players quickly put up their hands and gave their estimates.

"Eighty-five percent," one girl called.

"I'd say ninety," another speculated.

Still, a third said, "I don't know, but it's a lot."

"You're right. We don't know the exact number, but it's high. What you're thinking and feeling makes a huge difference in how you play. Now, let me ask you this. How much time does the average team spend on mental game training?"

The girls grew silent, most of them looking around the room. No one was quite sure what to say.

"Hmm, I'm guessing probably not much," the coach said with wide eyes and a small smile.

"That doesn't make much sense, does it? It's like if we said that hitting is important, but never took batting practice. We are going to start changing that right now.

"She's right, isn't she? Not too many players or coaches really think about it. It's as if we're supposed to figure it out on our own," Zoe said quietly to Ava. "I wouldn't have known anything at all if you hadn't taught me. I can't wait to see what else I can learn today."

Ava smiled at her friend's enthusiasm.

Coach Green walked down the center aisle and smiled at the girls. "The first thing I want you to do is get a partner. As we go through the booklet, you and your partner will sometimes work as a team. Are you ready to get started?" she asked as she walked back to the whiteboard in front.

"Yeah!" the girls responded.

46

The mental game is about getting yourself as ready as you can to win the next pitch. Does anyone understand what I mean by that?" Coach Green asked as she surveyed the room.

Ava's hand shot into the air: "It means that you have to be completely focused on the next pitch, no matter what just happened. You can't be thinking about a past mistake or get distracted by what's going on around you."

"Perfect! Great softball is played one pitch at a time. Sometimes during a game, bad things are going to happen. What matters most is how you react to those things. Players with a great mental game quickly bounce back and are ready to win the next pitch.

Coach Green then said, "On the first page of your booklet, I'd like you to write: 'The mental game is all about winning the next pitch. Win that next pitch!' I want you to be as creative as you can! Make it as big and as colorful as you want!"

The room was alive with activity as the girls worked diligently on the assignment. They laughed and chatted, filling the room with positive energy.

"I'm going to turn my paper sideways and use yellow and black for the Sting colors!" Zoe said as she sorted through the markers.

"Great idea! I'm going to draw a picture of a big softball with the words inside," Ava added.

Coach Green walked around the room, marveling at the creativity. She noticed Kayla's handiwork was less than impressive. She merely wrote the words in pencil on her paper without putting in much effort.

I think you can do better than that," the coach said with a slight frown. Kayla picked up some markers and pretended like she was going to color the page, but she stopped as soon as the coach walked away.

"I win the next pitch by smashing the ball. Nothing really ever goes wrong for me during a game. It's called having skill," she said under her breath to her teammate, Chloe. "Who needs this?"

Her teammate grabbed a red marker and wrote: "Kayla has skillz," and the girls giggled.

When all the girls finished, Coach Green said, "Nice work! That's our slogan for the day and your slogan for the season. Win the next pitch!"

"But how do you do that?" one of the Shark players said, tilting her head in confusion. "It seems really hard because when I miss a ball or the other team is beating us, I start doubting myself, and end up making more mistakes."

Several other players nodded.

"What a great question!" Grabbing a blue marker, Coach Green wrote, "In Order to Win the Next Pitch, You Must Have an Arrows-Out Attitude."

She then said, "It's frustrating when things don't go our way during a softball game. Isn't it? Sometimes we make mistakes; sometimes umpires miss calls, and sometimes the other team starts beating us. When that happens, it can feel like everything is against us. We feel like moping and pouting. All the energy is gone, and we feel like just giving up. That is called having an Arrows-In attitude. It's natural to feel this way when things don't go well, but it doesn't help you play better, so you have to make the choice to play Arrows-Out instead."

"What does Arrows-Out mean?" A Wolves player in the front row asked.

Coach Green gave a nod to one of her college players, who said, "Arrows-Out means all your energy is going out towards the game. No matter what bad things have happened in a game, you don't mope or pout; but keep trying. You put in extra effort on the next pitch. You stay positive and encourage your what."

Coach Green then wrote on the board. "You play each pitch like it's the first pitch of that game."

"When the first pitch of the game is made, no one is moping or pouting. There is so much focus, energy, and confidence. That's what we want each of you to do on every pitch of every game," the coach continued.

One of the college players added, "Players and teams that play Arrows-Out are hard to beat because they never, ever quit. They simply keep working hard in order to win the next pitch. Like Coach Green said, there's no moping, pouting, or throwing temper tantrums. It's attacking the next pitch with everything you have!"

The young players leaned forward as they hung on every word.

"Always playing Arrows-Out is something each of you can control," Coach Green added.

"You can choose how to react when things aren't going well. You don't have to stay Arrows-In. I can tell you from years and years of coaching that your Arrows-Out attitude will be noticed and admired by coaches, fans, teammates, and even your opponents! So, starting right now, I want all of you to become Arrows-Out players!"

She continued, "To help us remember Arrows-In and Arrows-Out, we're going to do something fun. I want you and your partner to think of a way to remember to play Arrows-Out rather than Arrows-In. It can be anything you want. We'll take ten minutes, and then some of you can share your ideas with us."

The room hummed again as the girls turned to their partners and got to work.

"What should we do?" Zoe asked Ava. "Should we draw a picture or something like that?"

"Hmm, it looks like a lot of people are drawing pictures. Let's do something different," Ava said as she rested her chin in her hand.

Zoe paused and looked toward the ceiling. "Oh! I've got it. Let's do a chant. The Sting can use it as a reminder when things go wrong!" she exclaimed with glee.

I can. Great idea. It has to be something catchy. Okay, let's see what we can come up with."

The girls hurriedly scribbled down ideas, crossing out some and circling others. Ava glanced at Kayla and her partner, Chloe. She could see they just wrote "Arrows-In" with a big X through it and "Arrows-Out" with "yes" next to it. The girls were on their phones now, watching a video and giggling.

After a few minutes, Zoe said, "I think we've got it!"

"Me, too!" Ava squealed, and the girls, who were very happy, quietly repeated their chant.

"We don't mope! We don't pout! We just play Arrows-Out!"

"Okay, times up!" Coach Green said. "Who wants to share first?"

A couple girls from the Wolves showed their picture of two softball players, one who was looking sad and playing Arrows-In and another who was confident and playing Arrows-Out.

A couple of other girls also showed off their Arrows-Out artwork, much to the delight of the group.

"Is there anyone else?" Coach Green asked, chin raised.

Zoe looked at Ava and raised her eyebrows.

Ava spoke up, "We decided to write a chant as a reminder."

"Let's hear it!" the coach said, a big smile on her face.

Ava and Zoe chanted, "We don't mope! We don't pout! We just play Arrows-Out!"

"Great!" Coach Green said. She picked up a marker and wrote it on the board. She and the college players repeated the chant, and soon the whole room was chanting, "We don't mope! We don't pout! We just play Arrows-Out!"

We don't mope!
We don't pout!
We just play!
ARROWS-OUT!

The chant was so simple, yet so powerful. Ava and Zoe nudged each other and beamed.

"Congratulations to everyone! I really liked what you came up with. Now, we'll remember that no matter what happens, we will always play…"

"Arrows-Out!" the girls shouted while the less than enthusiastic Bandits mockingly whispered the phrase.

"Well, let's take a ten-minute break, and then we will learn about self-talk," Coach Green said.

The players got up and moved around the room, some going into the hallway and others sharing their creations with their teammates and players from other teams.

"They liked our chant, didn't they?" Zoe asked as she got up and put her arm around Ava.

55

"Yeah, it's catchy," Ava said with a grin before she broke into the chant once more.

"We don't mope! We don't pout! We just play Arrows-Out!"

"Hey, Sting! Nice chant. Oh, wait, no, it's not," Kayla said as she walked by. "I can't wait to play you girls. If you call it playing. I'm sure there'll be more pouting and moping, just like last year," she mockingly predicted, tilting her chin up. "Bandits let's go get a drink, and we can work on our own chant. It'll say something like, 'The Sting got stung.'" The Bandits laughed as they followed Kayla out the door.

"Oh, they make me so mad," Zoe said with a scowl, her face reddening.

"It's okay, let them trash talk. We'll just play our best tomorrow and see what happens," Ava replied. "Let's meet up with Addie, Sophia, and the rest of the girls."

Zoe and Ava soon found Coach Moore and the other Sting players gathered at the far end of the hall.

56

I love your chant, Ava and Zoe!" Addie said enthusiastically as they joined the group. "I think we should use it this season. Coach, what do you think?"

"I agree! We can make it our mission to play Arrows-Out all the time. If something bad happens, we'll keep playing hard to win the next pitch. With that attitude, we'll be tough to beat no matter what," the coach said as she and the girls exchanged high-fives.

"I'm proud of you girls for wanting to learn the mental side of softball, so you can become better players. Most girls your age don't understand how important it is. You'll see how much better you play, how much better we play this year. Now, let's head back in!" Coach Moore said. The group marched down the hall, full of energy and optimism.

5

What You Say to Yourself Matters

"Okay everyone, take a seat, and we'll begin. I'm going to have two of my college players speak to you about the importance of self-talk in the final part of today's clinic. Take it away, ladies." Coach Green gestured toward the players standing to her right.

"Hi, my name is Emily Placie, and I'm Coastal's starting catcher," a young woman wearing a teal and white Coastal University T-shirt began.

"And I'm Macy Richardson and play center field for the team. I see the Wolves are here today. Here's an interesting fact: Emily and I both played for the Wolves when we were your age," she beamed with delight, the corners of her eyes crinkling.

Zoe noticed the Wolves, who were sitting in the front rows, exchange surprised, excited glances.

Emily continued. "Macy and I are going to teach you something very important. So far today, you've learned that playing softball is all about getting ready to win the next pitch, right?"

"Right," the girls agreed.

"We also learned that when things aren't going well, you have to make the decision to play Arrows-Out rather than Arrows-In. Right?" Emily asked.

"Right!" exclaimed the crowd once more.

"One easy way to know if you're Arrows-Out or Arrows-In is to listen to what you're saying to yourself. It's called self-talk. Does anyone know what self-talk is?"

Addie's hand was the first that shot into the air, and Emily pointed to her. "Yes, young lady, care to take a guess?"

Addie sat up straight, speaking with confidence. "It's that voice inside your head that talks to you every day. It's like we tell ourselves what we need to do, how we feel, and if we are doing something right or not."

"You got it. And did you know that what you tell yourself affects how you feel? For example, if I miss a ball and tell myself, 'You always mess up, Emily,' I'll feel sad and down. If, on the other hand, I say, 'It's okay; I'll get the next one,' I won't feel as bad, and I'll be ready for the next pitch.

Macy jumped in, "So, learning to control what you say to yourself is a skill, just like hitting, pitching, and fielding. Like most players after a mistake, my self-talk is immediately negative, so I have to become aware of it and change it. When we first came to Coastal University, Coach Green taught us the rules of positive self-talk. Emily and I are going to teach you those same rules. They are known as the Four Ss."

"In your packet, there's a sheet with four letter Ss going down the page. As we go, fill in the blanks," Emily instructed.

Zoe couldn't help but notice Kayla scribbling something on her paper and showing it to the other

Bandits, who started giggling. Zoe elbowed Ava and nodded in the direction of the Bandits.

Kayla glanced over and held up her paper. She had written, "Sting the Sting!" on each of the four Ss.

"You're funny," Zoe said, shaking her head in disgust. "I think you should pay attention. You might learn something."

"We already know everything we need to know to beat you," Kayla said with a sly grin. "Not that beating you takes much."

"Listen up, girls," Coach Green gently told them as she noticed the exchange.

Emily wrote: "Say Something Positive," in big green letters on the board.

"When something goes wrong, it's easy to have negative self-talk. It happens almost automatically. But as a player, you can catch it and change it to positive self-talk. Doing that will not only make you feel better but also help you play better.

"Like, what should we say?" a Shark player asked.

"I say a lot of positive things to myself before during, and after the game. I might say something like going to play my best.'" Emily paused to smile at the girls before continuing.

"If I make a good play or have a good at-bat, during the game my self-talk might be, 'Great job!' 'I knew I could do it.' 'Way to go, Emily!' After an error or a bad at-bat, I might say, 'I'll get the next one.' 'I'm still a good hitter.' 'Time to make a great play,' or 'She got me this time, but next time I'll crush it,'" Emily explained.

"Telling yourself something positive is the same T in the Three Ts of resetting that you taught me," Zoe whispered to Ava. "It's just that you do it more often. I never thought of doing it before the game to get ready to play my best."

"Me neither!" Ava replied.

Emily went on, "After a game, I try to remember all the good plays I made and my good at-bats. I even make up a quick video in my head of those plays and at-bats. So, I might say, 'You really smacked that ball the first time up.' 'Great job!'"

"While I'm saying that to myself, I am replaying a video of it and thinking about how good it felt," she said, gesturing with her hands.

Macy added, "I do the same thing. Last game, I made a diving catch, and on the way home, I made sure to tell myself positive things about that play. I kept going over that catch in my head. I also do it before I fall asleep at night. I think about my good plays and at-bats over and over. It really boosts my confidence."

Emily nodded, then her eyebrows drew together as her gaze swept the group in front of her. "Girls, this next point is very important. After making a mistake, you don't want to replay that mistake over and over in your mind because that will hurt your confidence. Do the Three Ts to reset, and no replaying the mistake!"

Macy told the girls to flip the page over and write down what they will say to themselves before, during, and after a game. When they were done, she asked, "Anyone want to share their self-talk before the game?"

"I'm going to say, 'Nothing is going to stop me today!'" suggested one of the Wolves.

I'll say, 'I can't wait to play great today,'" a girl wearing a Sharks jersey offered.

"Very good! Now, what are things you ladies might say to yourself following an error?"

Macy pointed to Sophia, who said, "'Mistakes happen.' 'You're still a good first baseman.' 'You got this!'"

Sophia smiled, then added, "If I had a bad at-bat, I'd say, 'No, problem. You're a good hitter.' 'Remember, it just takes one pitch. All you have to do is beat the pitcher once.' 'You can do it!'"

"Perfect!" Emily shouted with enthusiasm.

Macy jumped in, "It's also very important to use positive self-talk after you play well. I make sure to pat myself on the back for the good things that happened. I might say, 'Way to go, Macy!' or 'You played great!' It helps build confidence."

"That's right! Saying something good to yourself also helps you play Arrows-Out," Emily added as she grabbed a marker and walked towards the board. "Say something positive!" she said as she underlined the statement. "I think you girls have the first 3 down. Great job!"

"The next S is 'Shred the Arrows-In Words,'" the college player said as she wrote the phrase on the board.

"Remember that from now on we're all going to play Arrows-Out? To help us do that, we must learn to get rid of the Arrows-In phrases that pop into our minds. I say we picture a big paper shredder and shred Arrows-In phrases," Emily continued.

"What do you mean? What are Arrows-In phrases?" Addie asked with a puzzled look on her face.

Macy said, "Here are some examples," and turned and quickly listed some Arrows-In phrases on the board.

I can't.

I won't be able to do it.

I stink.

We can't win.

I should just give up.

Addie's hand shot into the air.

Yes. Macy said, pointing toward the Sting second baseman.

"I remember saying those things in a game last year. We were down five runs, and it was only the first inning. Saying those things made me want to give up. Does everyone say things like that to themselves when things aren't going right?"

"Great question! Yes. Arrows-In self-talk happens automatically, so it's important to catch it right away and shred it! See a video of you putting that thought in a big shredder. Add some of your positive self-talk phrases to get back to focusing on winning the next pitch."

The Coastal center fielder continued, "Arrows-In phrases drain your confidence and energy. If you say to yourself, 'I can't hit this girl,' you'll feel nervous and unsure. You won't play your best. The same is true for the whole team. Saying, 'We can't win,' when you fall behind in a game is an Arrows-In phrase. It's even harder to come back and win the game. So, when those phrases come into your mind, you get rid of them right away. Shred them in the shredder!"

Emily stepped to the board and filled in the next S. "Say what you *want* to have happen, not what you're *afraid* might happen! This is important because it changes how you feel and the kinds of pictures or videos you see in your mind. Let's say you're up to bat and the bases are loaded with two outs. If you said to yourself, 'Don't strike out,' what kind of video would you see in your mind? You'd see yourself striking out, right? That'll make you more nervous and hurt your confidence."

instead, in that situation, I want you to say something like, 'Hit the ball hard.' After saying that, what video do you see? It's completely different. I bet you'll notice a big difference in how you feel. You'll feel more powerful and confident. So, teach yourself to always say what you want to have happen instead of what you're afraid of!" Emily said with a big smile.

Macy added, "It's the same thing for pitchers. Instead of, 'Don't walk her,' say something like, 'Hit your spot,' or 'Throw your strike.' It makes a huge difference in your confidence."

Say what you WANT to have happen instead of what you're AFRAID might happen.

✗ NO	✓ YES
Don't Strikeout	Hit the Ball Hard
Don't Walk Her	Throw Your Strike
Don't Miss The Next Ball	Make a Great Play on The Next Ball

Macy finished the last S on the board, saying, "Support your teammates with positive self-talk. When things don't go as planned, good teammates pick each other up. Let your teammates know you are behind them, and this will help them stay positive and play Arrows-Out. So, girls, those are the Four Ss of self-talk. Remember, what you say to yourself matters!"

The girls sat down in their chairs, and Coach Green walked to the front of the room. "It's so important to watch how you talk to yourself. Using positive self-talk is a mental game skill that will help you play your best. Keep working on it."

The coach turned to her college players and said, "Thanks, ladies, for sharing this with us."

She then added, "That's the end of today's clinic. I'm glad you all came, and I hope you all learned a lot. Tomorrow, there will be a single elimination tournament. The Bandits will play the Sharks at 9:00am, and the Sting will play the Wolves at 11:30am. The winners will then play for the championship."

There was an instant buzz from the players. This tournament was going to be exciting.

Coach Green finished by saying, "I want to thank Emily and Macy for helping today. I hope each of you learned a lot, and we hope to see you at our Coastal University games."

Emily and Macy high-fived Coach Green before Emily said, "Keep working on that mental game. Watch that self-talk, and always play Arrows-Out!"

As they were heading toward the door, Emily and Macy stopped and looked back before starting to chant, "We don't mope! We don't pout! We just play Arrows-Out!" Coach Green and the group joined in as the girls continued to repeat the chant as the Coastal players made their way into the hallway. Zoe and Ava looked at each other, their cheeks lifted in a triumphant smile.

Zoe, Ava, and the rest of the Sting gathered their things and moved to the parking lot to wait for their rides.

"That was so much fun," Ava said, swinging her bag of gear cheerfully.

"Yeah, but how do you still have energy?" Zoe yawned. "I'm wiped!"

"Too wiped out for a sleepover?" Ava asked playfully.

Zoe grinned. "Never! Your house?"

Ava nodded. "My mom texted and said I could have a couple of girls over, and she'll drive us back here tomorrow."

"Awesome! I'll check with my mom. Who else is coming?" Zoe asked.

"Don't know yet. Hold on," Ava said. Then she ran up and tapped the shoulders of Addie and Sophia.

"Hey, you guys down for a sleepover at my house? My mom will drive us back here tomorrow for the tournament."

The girls' eyes lit up before Addie pulled out her phone and said, "I'd love it! Let me ask my parents."

"I'm in! I'll ask, too," Sophia said.

"Awesome! Girls' night sleepover!" Zoe squealed.

Zoe and Ava high-fived Addie and Sophia. Just then, they heard a familiar laugh behind them.

Aw, a sleepover," Kayla said sarcastically. "How cute! Hey, Bandits, what do you guys think the little Sting girls will be doing during their sleepover?"

"They'll do their nails. They might as well because they never hit the ball hard enough to chip a nail anyway," Chloe chimed in as she held her hands out as if she was admiring her nails.

"Maybe they'll be learning new chants about what it's like to lose to us again," another Bandit, Alexis Jones, offered.

"They could play two truths and a lie. The Sting can't play, the Sting mope and pout, and the Sting have never lost to the Bandits. Which one is the lie?" Kayla mocked Zoe's voice and laughed.

Zoe turned beet red and started to march toward the Bandits, but Ava grabbed her arm and held her back.

"Just ignore them, Zoe. Look, there's your mom's car."

As Zoe turned away, Kayla mumbled, "Coward."

Zoe whirled around, mouth open, ready to yell when her mom honked.

"Hurry up, Zoe!" her mom called from her open window.

"Come on, Zoe." Addie pulled on Zoe's arm. "Let's just go."

"Yeah, I need to ignore those idiots. Let's go have a sleepover," Zoe muttered, walking toward the car, glancing over her shoulder at the Bandits.

"See you tomorrow! Sweet dreams!" Kayla squawked as she and her teammates giggled.

***

"The pizza is ready!" Ava's mother called out from the kitchen.

"Great! I'm starving. Let's go!" Zoe said, stopping mid-dance. She and the other girls scrambled into the kitchen. After they finished eating, they kept dancing, giggling, and giving Oliver lots of attention until Ava's mom said, "You girls better get some rest. You have a big day ahead of you tomorrow."

"Your mom's right. We better get some sleep," Zoe said, spreading her sleeping bag out on the floor. Soon, the floor was covered with sleeping bags, and Oliver walked from one to the next, trying to get

...ection from anyone who would pay attention to him. After talking for a while, the girls fell into a comfortable silence. Oliver's quiet purring and the buzz of the nightlight on Ava's desk filled the room.

Addie broke the silence.

"Is anyone else worried about the Bandits? We're probably going to play them tomorrow, right?"

"Yeah," Zoe said, "but try not to worry about it."

"Are you worried, though?" Addie insisted.

Zoe sighed. "I'm not worried...more like mad. They're bad sports. They're good, and they know it. They don't respect the other teams they play."

"But they are good," Sophia added. "You have to admit."

"Yeah, they've got to be one of the best teams at the clinic," Addie said.

"If not *the* best team there," Sophia amended.

"Come on, guys," Ava said, scratching Oliver's chin. "We're a great team. We'll use what we've learned and make sure, no matter what, we're ready to win the next pitch. It's all about focusing on each pitch and not the Bandits. Right?"

The girls mumbled their agreement, and Ava sighed.

"Why don't we get some sleep, so we're ready tomorrow?" she suggested. "Oh, and another thing. We don't mope. We don't pout. We just play Arrows Out!"

The girls repeated the chant and giggled.

"Go, Sting!" Addie added.

Soon, the only sounds were the soft whirl of a ceiling fan and the rumble of Oliver's purring.

6

The Wolves are Howling

'I'm glad we didn't have to play the first game today," Ava said, crawling out of her sleeping bag.

"Me too," Sophia said, rubbing her eyes. "It's going to take a while for me to wake up."

"Not us! Wake up, everyone!" Zoe and Addie exclaimed. They were already up, dressed, and standing by their rolled-up sleeping bags.

"Today is tournament day. I can't wait!" Addie said as she bounced on the balls of her feet.

Zoe grabbed her batting helmet and gazed at the aggressive Sting logo while the girls watched. Her eyes narrowed as she tried to summon her own fierce expression. But she couldn't stop the grin from spreading across her face. Everyone burst out laughing.

The Sting players dressed and made their way downstairs where Ava's mother made sure they had a good breakfast and had them double-check they had everything they needed for the day.

"Okay, let's go," Ava said, motioning toward the door.

The girls loaded the trunk with their gear and climbed inside the car.

I've never played on a college field before. It's going to be so exciting. Are you girls ready to play?" Ava inquired.

"I'm excited, but I'm also nervous. We'll have to play the Bandits for the championship if we both win our first games. They're just so good it's scary," Addie said, biting her lower lip.

The mood turned serious as Zoe and Sophia listened with raised eyebrows.

"Let's not worry about that yet. We've got to focus on beating the Wolves first. Remember, we're good too. We simply need to be mentally tough today. Let's go over what we learned about the mental game yesterday." Ava surveyed the group and saw heads nodding in agreement.

Addie jumped in. "I'll go first. The most important pitch in any game is the next one. You've got to make sure you are ready for it. Can't be thinking about a bad play or a bad swing."

"And how do you do that?" Ava asked with the tone of a schoolteacher.

You use the Three I's to reset," Addie replied confidently.

"Great, what else?" Ava inquired.

Zoe's hands gripped an imaginary bat. "Use your pre-pitch routine with the focal point between each pitch. You'll see the ball from her hand all the way to the plate, and then, wham! You smash it!"

"You've got it! Finally, remember that if things aren't going your way, make sure to always play Arrows-Out and keep playing hard. No moping!" Ava lectured while waving her finger.

A spontaneous chant filled the car. "We don't mope! We don't pout! We just play Arrows-Out!"

"I love that," Ms. Davis said, smiling in her rearview mirror. She joined the group in another round of the chant, and the girls whooped in response.

As they pulled up to the softball field and got out of the car, the Sting players felt a mixture of anticipation and nerves. The air buzzed with excitement. Suddenly, Zoe heard a loud roar from the stands. She turned around to see a few Bandit players running around the bases while their fans cheered and

...ened. Her heart sank a bit as she glanced at the scoreboard. Bandits 8, Sharks 0.

Great, just great. The Bandits are going to win, she thought, stifling a frown. She noticed Addie staring at the scoreboard too.

"Girls! Girls! We're over here," Coach Moore's familiar voice boomed as she and the rest of the Sting players stood to the right of the backstop.

Zoe, Ava, Addie, and Sophia hustled over to the group.

"This game is about over, so let's go over there and start warming up," the coach said, pointing to a large open area of grass down the right-field line.

Excitement filled the air as the girls raced toward the large area to begin their warm-ups. They could see the Wolves doing the same thing across the field. The Wolves, wearing maroon jerseys and black pants, were spread out and enthusiastically throwing to each other.

"What do you know about the Wolves?" Ava asked, pausing to adjust her ponytail. "Are they good?"

Yeah, they are." Zoe scrunched her brow. "Maddy Parker, their pitcher, is the one to keep an eye on. She's got speed and throws strikes. We didn't play them last year, but we did see them play in a few tournaments. We've got some strong hitters, and it'll be a good game."

"You're right. We just have to play it one pitch at a time, like the coaches said. I'm excited for the challenge," Ava stated confidently as she slid her glove back on.

"Let's go, Sting!" Zoe replied with a nod.

Soon, the first game ended. The Bandits had won. This put them in the tournament championship game. As the Bandits celebrated their win, the Sting stopped throwing, gathered their things, and headed for the dugout.

"Look at them. Do you see how they're shaking hands with the Sharks? They're just rushing through the line and ignoring them. Poor sports!" Zoe muttered.

"They are, but let's not worry about them. We've got a game to play," Ava said.

82

Kayla, Chloe, and a few Bandit players left the dugout as the Sting were making their way in.

"Zoe! Good luck. We'll be rooting for you. We'd LOVE to play you for the championship. I want another ring," Kayla said with a smirk.

Zoe walked on, ignoring the comment as she pounded a softball into her glove. Kayla's remarks only fueled her fire.

The Wolves would bat first. Emma Lopez was the Sting's starting pitcher. The tall, lanky right-hander had a great fastball and an effective changeup. As she warmed up, the sound of her pitches smacking the catcher's mitt echoed across the diamond. The stands were packed with fans settling into their seats.

Grace Fredriks, the Wolves' leadoff hitter, stepped up to the plate. Strands of blond hair peeked from the bottom of her batting helmet. With a fierce look in her eye, she readied herself for the first pitch.

"All right, Emma! Let's go! You can do it!" Zoe yelled and hit her glove with the palm of her open hand.

Throw your game!" Addie added as she gingerly bounced out at second base.

"Play ball!" barked the umpire as he crouched behind home plate.

The first pitch of the game was straight down the middle. Grace clenched her teeth and swung aggressively. She made solid contact, and a sudden hush fell over the crowd. It was a long fly ball to dead center. Mia dashed back but ran out of room as the ball sailed over the fence for a home run. The crowd erupted in cheers as Grace rounded the bases with a triumphant smile.

Zoe, Ava, and Addie jogged to the mound to talk with Emma.

"No problem. Do your reset, and let's win this next pitch," Ava said as she hit Emma's leg with her closed mitt. "You got this!"

Emma took a deep breath as she walked to the back of the pitching circle. To get rid of the last pitch she wiped the back of her glove down her leg. The Sting infielders heard their tall pitcher say, "You're a tough pitcher, Emma. Nobody hurt. Throw your game! Emma's face filled with determination as she turned toward home plate to face the next batter.

"Steeerike! Steeerike! Steeerike! Steeerike!" was all he umpire said for the rest of that inning. The focused ;ting pitcher quickly struck out the next three Wolves.

"Okay, let's hit," Coach Moore said before eading off the batting order. "This pitcher is tough, but you're good hitters. Do your pre-pitch routine and ocus on the release point. Nothing else matters. We'll core some runs!"

The Wolves sprinted to their positions, full of :nergy. Maddy Parker started throwing her warm-up pitches. Dozens of eyes from the Sting bench quietly ;awked at the right-hander as she grunted and vindmilled the yellow softball towards home plate.

Whoosh! Smack!

Whoosh! Smack!

Whoosh! Smack!

"She's the fastest pitcher I've ever seen in my life!" Addie bit her lower lip and whispered to Grace as they .tood in the on-deck circle.

"Yeah, it's a blur," Grace agreed, nodding.

85

"Play ball!" the umpire shouted and waved in hand towards Addie, who was taking a few last-minute practice swings beside home plate.

Addie walked nervously toward the plate, her bat swaying in her right hand. Both teams' fans yelled encouragement to their players.

Addie stepped into the box and took a quick practice swing. Maddy went into her windup and slung the first pitch toward home. Addie saw the ball leave the pitcher's hand, and then it was gone.

Whizz!

Addie seemed frozen in time, not even blinking.

"Strike one!" the umpire yelled.

Wow, I didn't even see that one. Addie thought as a sudden sense of doom overtook her.

"You can do it! Hit it right up the middle!" Coach Moore called to the young hitter from the third-base coach's box as she clapped her hands.

Addie noticed her now-pounding heart. She took her practice swings, but they seemed to be a bit more uncertain. Maddy's next pitch sped through the air and

86

right into the catcher's mitt. Addie started to swing, but it was too late. The ball flew past her.

"Strike two!" boomed the umpire.

Addie's mind raced. Every sound around the ballpark rushed over her like an ocean wave.

"You got this!" Sophia called out. "You're a good hitter, Addie! You can do it!"

A few people in the stands instructed the anxious hitter, trying to make their advice heard above the others.

"Look for a strike and hit it!" encouraged one parent.

"Relax up there!" called out another.

"Be confident!" another suggested.

Addie scanned both dugouts and looked at the fans before stepping back in. Her stomach was in knots, and her chest tightened.

Her thoughts danced wildly. *If it's a strike, I've got to hit it. I just have to! Don't strike out! Don't strike out!*

Maddy got her sign from the catcher and let the ball fly. The softball nose-dived into the dirt about three feet in front of the plate, but Addie swung anyway. She didn't even wait to see where the ball was going before swinging. The Wolves' catcher scooped up the ball and tagged Addie on the back of her jersey.

"That wasn't good." Addie sighed as she walked into the dugout. "I was so nervous that I completely forgot to do my pre-pitch routine. Instead of being relaxed and focused, it just got worse with each pitch. I also said, 'Don't strike out,' instead of, 'Hit the ball hard.' That at-bat was a mess!"

"You'll remember next time, and you'll get your hit. Now, remember it's Arrows-Out," Zoe said with a soft smile and nudged the Sting second baseman with her elbow.

"Arrows-Out it is," Addie said. "Let's go, Gracie!" She stood and clapped.

Addie wasn't alone in her struggle to hit the Wolves' ace pitcher. Grace and Sophia also struck out with neither batter seeing more than four pitches. Three up and three strikeouts.

Even though three of their best hitters just struck out without so much as hitting a foul ball, the Sting weren't discouraged. They grabbed their masks and

litts and sprinted to their positions. No moping. No
outing. They were undoubtedly playing Arrows-Out.

Emma and Maddy continued to dominate the
hitters over the next four innings. The scoreboard still
read: Wolves 1, Sting 0. Both teams had a hard time
hitting the ball, and when they did, the defenses
responded by making every play. Despite the lack of
runs, the game remained intense because neither
pitcher was willing to give an inch. The tension in the
air crackled at an all-time high.

Before the top of the sixth inning, Coach Moore
called the team together. "Let's make this our inning.
Keep playing great defense, and we'll win this thing!"

The Sting took the coach's words to heart. With a
renewed sense of energy and confidence, they broke
the huddle shouting, "One-two-three! Go, Sting!"

Emma finished her warmup tosses, but it seemed
her fastball had lost some of its steam. Kristen James,
the Wolves' third baseman, smashed a line drive single
to left to start the inning. Callie Frazier, the speedy
centerfielder, slapped an infield hit that Zoe couldn't
get to. The Wolves had a rally going.

Time! Coach Moore called to the umpire and jogged to the pitcher's circle. Ava, Zoe, and the rest of the infielders joined her. "They might try to bunt, so infielders, be ready. Keep throwing strikes, Emma, and we'll get out of this inning," the coach said before hustling back to the dugout.

The other infielders went back to their positions but Ava lingered in the circle.

"I'm really going to cheat in from third. If she bunts and pops it up, I'll grab it," Ava confidently whispered to Emma.

"I'm going to throw it high and inside then." Emma nodded as she covered her mouth with her glove.

The Wolves' third-base coach went through the signs to the next batter, Kyra Reed. As Coach Moore predicted, it was a bunt. Emma threw the pitch right where she wanted it—high and inside. Kyra squared to bunt, reached up, and made contact. The ball popped up in the air, where it seemed to hang forever.

"Back, back, back!" screamed the third-base coach to the runners.

Ava dove for the ball and hit the ground hard.

"Uuuhg!" she cried out as she skidded across the turf. The ball fell into her mitt. By the time she struggled to her feet, both runners had safely scampered back to their bases.

"Great play! Way to go, Ava!" Zoe said as she pumped her fist. "One out!"

"Just like we planned it." Ava winced as she tossed the ball back to Emma. "Now, let's get the next one out."

The Sting had work to do to get out of the inning. Wolves' powerful cleanup hitter, Brystol Saylor, was up next. Brystol, the biggest kid on the team, towered over the Sting's catcher and stood eye-to-eye with the home-plate umpire. She confidently strolled up to the plate, her eyes narrowing in determination.

Whoosh!

Whoosh!

Whoosh!

She took three powerful warm-up swings that crisply cut through the air, creating a noticeable breeze.

"Outfielders! Give her a step!" yelled Coach Moore as she exited the dugout and hastily pushed her arms in front of her.

The Sting outfielders quickly heeded the coach's warning.

While most in the crowd shouted words of encouragement at the top of their lungs, some sat nervously on the edge of their seats. The fans anticipated something big, and so did Zoe.

"Make your pitch, Emma. You got this!" Zoe called above the noise of the crowd. She, too, took a step back at shortstop.

Brystol, teeth clenched, glared out toward the pitcher's circle, as if daring the Sting pitcher to throw her a strike. This was a chance to drive both runners home and break this game wide open.

Emma looked just as determined, her eyes focused on her catcher's target. The Sting infielders were ready to react to anything that came their way.

The umpire yelled, "Play ball!" and pointed toward the circle.

Emma got her sign and went into the windup. She fired her best fastball towards the inside corner of the plate. Brystol waited for it.

Crack!

A line-drive rocketed off her bat and whistled through the air - right at Ava.

Smack!

In the blink of an eye, she had the ball in her glove.

"Back, back, back!" the Wolves' coach was screaming, but it was too late.

The runner on second base was too far off the bag. Ava fired the ball to Addie at second for a double play.

"Out! Out!" the umpire yelled emphatically, pumping his right arm in the air.

The inning was over. Somehow, the Sting got out of the jam without the Wolves adding to their lead.

While the Southport fans cheered wildly, a hushed silence filled the Wolves' side of the bleachers. The Wolves players, too, stood stunned by the turn of events. Their faces showed a mix of disappointment and disbelief as they looked around, almost in slow motion.

"Great play, Ava!" Zoe said as she hopped up and down and grabbed Ava by her shoulder.

She and the rest of the Sting sprinted off the field with a renewed sense of optimism and energy.

"Fantastic play, Ava," Coach Moore said with a huge smile as she greeted the third baseman in the dugout. "Now, let's score some runs and win this thing!"

"Let's go, Sting!" Zoe exclaimed as she grabbed her bat and batting helmet. She was going to lead off the inning.

The Sting's final at-bat hovered on the edge. It was now or never. Maddy Parker's warm-up pitches popped the catcher's mitt with the same zip as they had earlier in the game.

As Zoe took her warm-up swings, she seemed unfazed by Maddy's crisp warm-up pitches. *I can get her. Look for a strike and hit the ball hard!* she thought as she adjusted her batting glove.

Zoe pushed down on the top of her helmet as she walked to the plate. She carefully did her pre-pitch routine and locked in on the release point. Even though the fans of both teams screamed, she didn't hear anything. It was just her and the ball coming out of the pitcher's hand. Nothing else mattered.

Maddy wound up and let the first pitch fly. It looked like it missed the plate outside, but the umpire called it a strike. Strike one. Zoe seemed unconcerned as she carefully did her pre-pitch routine and stepped back into the box.

The next pitch was a change-up. Zoe swung and tapped a soft foul over to the third base dugout. Strike two. Again, she did her pre-pitch routine.

"She looks confident up there, even with two strikes," Addie said to Ava without taking her eyes off Zoe.

"Yeah, she does. I love that she is just doing her routine and taking it one pitch at a time," Ava responded, staring intently towards the field.

Again, Zoe did the four-step routine and stepped into the box. Maddy's next pitch was heading toward the strike zone. Zoe swung and felt the bat vibrate.

The ground ball skipped across the turf towards the hole between shortstop and third.

"Run! Run! Run!" echoed from the stands as the shortstop backhanded it.

Faster! Faster! Faster! Zoe thought as she sprinted towards the first base bag, giving it her all. Her helmet bobbed on her head, nearly covering both eyes.

The shortstop's sharp throw was on target. It was going to be a close play.

Zoe felt her right foot hit the bag just before she heard the ball smack into the first baseman's glove.

"Safe!" the umpire called as he forcefully extended his arms. The Sting bench erupted in cheers. The tying run was on base.

"I made it," Zoe said as she tried to catch her breath. A huge smile filled the mask of her batting helmet.

"Great hustle!" Coach Green, who was coaching first base, said and gave Zoe a fist bump. "Way to get something started!"

With the Sting crowd and bench still filled with excitement, Lily bunted the first pitch. It was a perfect bunt, as four of the Wolves surrounded it but couldn't reach it in time. The Sting now had two on and nobody out.

Hannah King was up next. Coach Moore decided to let her hit rather than bunt. The Sting's catcher was one of their best power hitters. Like the other Sting players, Hannah carefully did her pre-pitch routine. She didn't notice the sweat rolling down the side of her face. She didn't hear the crowd. Hannah was locked into the pitcher's release point. It was just going to be the ball coming out of the hand. Nothing else mattered.

Maddy glared in at her catcher, wound up, and fired the pitch. Hannah swung and connected. A gasp went up in the crowd as the ball ricocheted off her bat sailing high to deep centerfield. Callie, the Wolves centerfielder, sprinted back and made an over-the shoulder catch before turning and firing the softball back towards the infield.

"Get over here! Get over here!" Coach Moore screamed to Zoe on second base.

Zoe tagged up and scrambled into third base.

"Stay right here. On the bag! On the bag!" Coach Moore screamed as she repeatedly pointed to third base.

Lily also tagged up and made it safely to second base. The Sting had the tying and winning runs in scoring position with one out. It was now up to Addie

"You can do it!" Zoe said as she stood on third base, clapping her hands.

"Get your hit!" Lily hollered from second, but her words drowned in the noise from the crowd.

Addie dropped the extra bat she was swinging and started walking to the plate. Her heart pounded, and her mind began to race. This was a big spot in a big game.

Whew! Don't strike out! she thought before suddenly stopping. Addie remembered what she learned at the clinic about self-talk. *Say what you want to have happen instead of what you are afraid will happen.*

"Wait! Hit the ball hard. You're a good hitter. See it and rip it!" Addie whispered to herself. She took a few extra deep breaths and continued her walk to home plate with a newfound sense of confidence.

"Get your base hit, Addie! You can do it!" Coach Moore clapped and nodded.

Addie took a deep breath, looked at her focal point, and then zeroed in on Maddy's release point. Even though the crowd and players from both teams were yelling nonstop, she didn't hear them. She was focused.

Maddy hurled a fastball towards her catcher's open mitt. The spinning softball was coming right down the middle. Addie saw it the whole way. It was like the game was in slow motion. She swung and felt the strong jolt of the bat in her hands. It was a line drive right over the pitcher's head. A base hit!

Zoe scored and watched as Coach Moore frantically waved Lily around third base. Lily hit the bag and stumbled a bit before righting herself. The throw from the outfield was on a line to the plate. The roar of the crowd was deafening. There was a slide. There was a tag.

"Safe!" rang out from the umpire. The Sting had won 2-1. The Sting's fans cheered feverishly.

The Sting players poured out of the dugout and sprinted to home plate and mobbed Lily and Addie.

Coach Moore ran to join the celebration of high fives and fist bumps. "Great job! Great job!"

Addie emerged from the group and headed towards the dugout. She glanced into the stands and saw her parents beaming with pride.

I did it! I did it! That at-bat felt so different. I was so relaxed and focused, she thought, almost in a state of stunned disbelief.

Walking back to the dugout, Zoe saw a familiar figure standing by the backstop.

Zoe, I'm surprised you won. Good game, I guess," Kayla said with a shoulder shrug. "I'm glad we get to play you for the championship. It'll be just like last year, and I'll be adding another ring to my collection."

Zoe lifted her chin and kept walking towards her teammates. "We'll just have to wait and see what happens."

7

Bring on the Bandits

"Take a look at them," Zoe scoffed as she gazed over at the third base dugout. "Instead of warming up, they're laughing and messing around. They think they've already won the championship."

Ava stopped throwing and looked across the field. She saw some of the Bandits laughing and making faces at each other as they made silly throws. "Let's just focus on our game and play our best. We're a good team, too. Last year was last year. This is this year. Let's win this championship!"

"Okay, everyone, come on in," Coach Moon called. She glanced down at her scorebook as the girls hustled into the dugout. "The game is going to start in five minutes. We're the home team, and our lineup is the same as last game, except Sophia is pitching instead of Emma. Hitters, it's all about winning the next pitch, so do your pre-pitch routine. What else did we learn at the clinic yesterday?"

"Have positive self-talk!" Addie answered with her eyebrows raised in encouragement.

"And always play Arrows-Out!" Ava added with a huge smile.

"You got it! We don't mope! We don't pout! We just play Arrows-Out!" the coach began, and the rest of the Sting joined in, their voices ringing across the field.

"We don't mope! We don't pout! We just play Arrows-Out!" They continued with the chant, which got louder and louder, until the players broke the huddle and sprinted to their positions.

"Let's go, girls. Nothing gets by this infield," Zoe said as she tapped gloves with Ava, Addie, and Emma behind the pitcher's circle.

Sophia's warm-up pitches hit their mark. The infielders fielded every warm-up grounder and fired strikes to first base. The outfielders sprinted to catch each other's throws. The Southport Sting were ready to play.

The same was not true for the Bandits. Their leadoff hitter, Chloe Wilson, sat in the dugout eating candy and laughing with some other players. Zoe noticed the rest of the Bandit players were also distracted. A few Bandit players were still behind the dugout, talking to people in the stands. Even their coaches were on their phones.

"Let's go. I need a batter!" the umpire called impatiently as he gestured towards the Bandits' dugout.

Only then did Chloe grab her bat and run to home plate without taking any warm-up swings.

Sophia's first pitch was a strike that Chloe watched zip by her. The second pitch was the same, and so was the third. Three pitches, three strikes, and she was out without even swinging once. Chloe grimaced and dropped the barrel of her bat as she slowly trudged towards the dugout.

Great job, Sophia! Way to throw those strikes!" Addie called from second base.

Ava took a few steps towards the circle and smacked the inside of her glove with the palm of her hand. "That's the way to start the game!"

Sophia nodded but kept a serious look on her face.

The next Bandit batter, Aubrey Brown, hit the first pitch into the air toward Addie at second base. Aubrey stood at home plate with her bat in hand, believing it would be an easy catch. Addie got under the ball, but it somehow popped out of her glove and landed at her feet. Shocked, she quickly picked it up and fired a perfect throw to Emma at first base to get the out. Aubrey, who wasn't running, was only three steps out of the batter's box. The Bandits' fans groaned loudly, and the Bandits' coaches frowned.

"Good recovery, Addie," Zoe said as she pointed to the still somewhat stunned Addie. Zoe then noticed that Addie used the Three Ts to reset.

Way to reset, Addie, Zoe thought as she watched the second baseman.

Sophia got the next Bandit batter out on strikes. The Sting energetically dashed off the field, eager to hit.

With long faces, the Bandits shuffled out to their positions. Kayla Pennington, the starting pitcher, picked up the softball and repeatedly slammed it into her glove.

"She's good, and she knows it." Zoe's forehead was scrunched as she watched Kayla throw her warm-up pitches.

"How good is she? I've never seen her pitch," Ava asked as she pulled her batting helmet out from under the bench.

"Well, let's just say that last year she pitched against us in all three games. We didn't get many hits, and I think she struck everyone out at least once. At another tournament, she threw two no-hitters," Zoe said, biting her lower lip and rubbing the side of her face.

Addie, who was usually nervous, spoke up. "That was last year. We're better this year for sure."

You're exactly right. You girls have practiced hard and have also learned a lot about the mental game. This is a new season," Coach Moore added.

Addie was the leadoff hitter. Kayla's first pitch was right down the middle. Addie gritted her teeth and swung only to find air. That fastball was past her before she knew it. After fouling two pitches off and watching a third bounce in, Addie hit a hard groundball to the shortstop, who made the play to get her out at first.

"Right on her," Zoe said to Addie as she walked past in the dugout.

"She's fast, but we can hit her," Addie replied as she pulled her helmet off. "Let's go, Grace. Get your hit!"

Grace made good contact as she hit a fly that was caught by the center fielder, Meg Dakin. Sophia ended the inning with a hard liner to second.

The score remained 0-0 for the next three innings. Neither team could get anything going through the first four innings. The Bandits managed just two hits and the Sting's only hit was a single by Ava. The crowd as on the edge of their seats, waiting for someone to break the deadlock.

In the top of the fifth, the Bandits' leadoff batter, Abbey Miller, smashed a groundball right between Addie at second and Emma at first. The next Bandit hitter bunted, but the ball popped up off her bat down the third-base line. Ava sprinted in and made a desperate dive, but the softball was just out of reach. The spinning ball dropped to the turf and rolled back towards home plate before stopping in fair territory.

Cheers from the crowd quickly turned to a hushed silence as Ava rolled on her back and grabbed her stomach, gasping for air. Coach Moore ran to her star player.

"Just relax. Don't get up. You had the wind knocked out of you. Just try to relax. You're okay." The coach crouched down and offered her help.

Ava took some deep breaths and slowly stood, still holding her stomach.

Coach Moore turned to the Sting bench. "Abigail! Abigail! Get your glove. You're in at third."

I'm okay. Ava winced, not wanting to leave the game.

"No, you're coming out. Let's go in, sit down, and take a break," the coach said as she put her arm on Ava's shoulder.

Zoe looked around at her teammates who were glued to their positions, watching Ava as she hobbled off field. The game itself suddenly seemed less important. Sophia and the rest of the Sting gazed into the dugout, watching to see what was happening with Ava.

"Play ball!" broke the silence on the field.

The Bandits had runners on first and second with no outs. This was their chance to break the tie. Sophia's first pitch sailed over her catcher's head and bounced hard off the backstop. Both Bandits raced to the next base without a throw.

"Reset, Sophia! Reset!" Zoe called from her shortstop position.

Sophia nodded and walked to the back of the circle, took some deep breaths, and refocused. The next pitch found the catcher's mitt as it screamed past hitter's bat. A four ball and then Sophia's best change-up of the day ended that at-bat with a much-needed strikeout. One out.

The next hitter, Stella Miles, scalded a groundball Abigail at third base. The hard-hit ball skipped off her shoulder and rolled into short left field. Grace sprinted in, but by the time she picked it up, both runners had scored. The Bandits led 2-0.

While the Bandits cheered wildly in the dugout, the Sting were deflated. This was a championship game that seemed lost.

Zoe took a few steps towards third. "Are you okay, Abby?"

"Yeah, it hurts, but I'm okay." She rolled her left shoulder and winced.

"Let's go, girls! Get an out!" Coach Moore yelled, trying to generate some enthusiasm. She didn't get much response other than some mumbled cheers said with sagging shoulders.

Fortunately for the Sting, the next two Bandits made outs. The first one was a popup to Hannah behind the plate, and the final out was an easy fly Mia in center field.

The Bandits, now full of energy, sprinted onto th field, racing past the Sting players, who trudged their dugout.

When they reached the dugout, everyone huddle around Ava.

"How are you feeling?" Addie asked, leanir forward in the group.

"Better. I feel a lot better. But, girls, you kno what I'm seeing? Arrows-In from everyone. It's n over. It's only 2-0. We can still win this game."

"She's right," Zoe said as she surveyed the group. "Just like we learned yesterday at the clinic. Arrows-In doesn't win games. Arrows-Out does. Let's keep attacking. Compete as hard as you can on every pitch that's left in this game."

With a slight smile, Ava stood up from the bench and joined the huddle. She stuck her hand in the middle. The other Sting players hurriedly scrambled to get their hands on top of hers.

"We don't mope! We don't pout! We just play Arrows-Out!" Ava began, and the other Sting players joined in, repeating the chant louder each time.

Kayla and the Bandits stopped warming up and seemed puzzled as the Sting broke the huddle with a renewed sense of enthusiasm.

Down 2-0, the Sting needed baserunners. Mia led off the inning by hitting a hard ground ball right at Chloe, the Bandits' second baseman. Chloe got in front of it, but it went right through her legs and into right field.

"Great! Just great!" Chloe barked, loud enough for everyone to hear. She checked her glove to see if, somehow, there was a hole in it.

Kayla glared at her.

"She needs to reset," Ava said to Addie as they watched Chloe smack her glove on the turf and stomp back to her position.

"Yeah, now look at her. She's really moping and pouting. Arrows-In for sure," Addie said as she chomped on her gum.

With Mia on first, Lily swung and missed at two strikes before doing her pre-pitch routine and calmly stepping back into the batter's box. Her third swing was a good one. The bat crisply cut through the air and connected with the yellow softball. It was another hard ground ball right to Chloe. The softball skipped up her arm and bounded into right field. Mia rounded second base but wisely scrambled back to the bag as the throw zipped back into the infield.

"C'mon, Chloe! I can't do it all myself. Get in the game," Kayla snapped as she shook her head and kicked the turf.

Chloe huffed, threw her head back, and stared at the sky.

The Sting had two runners on base without getting a hit.

"Now, it's Kayla who needs a reset. She's Arrows-In for sure," Addie said to Ava as they studied the Bandits' pitcher from the dugout.

"Yeah, she's out of control," Addie replied as she watched Kayla stomp around, still shaking her head.

With two runners on and no outs, Hannah stepped into the batter's box. The scowling Kayla wound up and flung her first pitch towards the plate. It was a little outside, and Hannah let it go by.

"Ball outside," was the call.

"That was a strike!" Kayla muttered as she got the ball back from her catcher.

The next pitch flew even more outside, and once again, Hannah wisely watched it zip by.

"Ball two," the umpire said to the dismay of the Bandits' pitcher.

"Again, another strike. I can't catch a break!" Kayla slammed the ball into her glove.

I'll show them. I'll throw this as hard as I can, she thought as she hurriedly stepped on the pitching rubber and threw the next pitch.

The pitch was fast, very fast, but it was wild. The ball sailed way over the catcher's head, all the way to the backstop. Both runners moved up a base. The Sting now had the tying run on second base.

"Don't walk her!" Chloe yelled as Kayla walked back from covering home plate.

"She should be saying, 'Throw your strikes,' instead of, 'Don't walk her,'" Sophia said to Emma. "You can tell they didn't pay attention to anything at the clinic."

Emma nodded in agreement.

Kayla shot a withering glare at Chloe before saying, "You just play second."

Once again, Kayla slammed the ball into her glove before stepping on the rubber and letting the next pitch go. It wasn't even close to a strike as the catcher dove outside to make a great block.

Ball four and the bases were loaded. Zoe was the next batter.

"Time! Time!" the Bandits' coach called to the umpire as she hurried from the dugout and called the infielders into the circle.

"The coach is trying to settle them down. Did you see her tell them to take some deep breaths?" Ava said. "They're in a jam. This is our chance to score some runs."

The meeting broke up, and it was time to play ball.

Hit the ball hard! You're a good hitter! You can do it! Zoe thought as she finished her warm-up swings and confidently marched to home plate.

The crowd cheered, louder than at any time in the game. The Bandits' bench chanted for their pitcher, while the Sting bench did the same for Zoe.

Zoe carefully did her pre-pitch routine. Even though everyone in the park was yelling, she didn't hear a thing. She wasn't thinking of anything. Zoe focused on the release point.

Kayla stared at her catcher. Gone was the confident smile Kayla had earlier in the game. She wiped her sweaty pitching hand down the side of her pant leg. With the bases loaded, she knew she had to throw strikes.

Kayla got her sign and windmilled the ball on a direct line towards her catcher's open mitt.

Zoe saw the spinning ball all the way to the plate and took a mighty swing. The ball connected with the sweet spot of her bat. Zoe's hands vibrated from the sudden jolt.

Whizz!

The softball screamed past a ducking Kayla before Zoe could even take a step out of the batter's box. It was a solid base hit to center field.

"Go, go, go!" Coach Moore yelled as she frantically waved both Mia and Lily around third base.

The Sting fans and bench erupted in cheers as both runners easily scored to tie the game at 2-2.

Hannah stopped at second as the center fielder made a strong throw to the shortstop. Zoe rounded first before returning to the bag. A wide smile stretched across her face. Her fingers could still feel the bat's vibration.

The Sting bench greeted Mia and Lily at home plate before turning their attention to Zoe at first.

"Great job!"

"Nice hit!"

"Way to go!"

Zoe gave a small fist pump into the air as she bounced excitedly on first base. She saw her parents cheering and clapping wildly in the stands.

A deflated Kayla didn't dare look at Zoe. With slumped shoulders, she made her way to the back of the pitcher's circle. The rest of the Bandits stood quietly, some with their hands on hips. Their stunned fans settled into a quiet daze.

Emma energetically approached the plate, knowing a base hit would give them the lead. Kayla's first pitch was high, but Emma eagerly swung and hit a popup to the third baseman for the first out of the inning.

Addie hit next and, after fouling off two pitches, hit an easy fly to left field that was caught. Both Sting runners had to hold their bases.

It seemed like Kayla was going to get out of the inning. She just had to get Grace out. Grace was a good hitter, so it wasn't going to be easy.

Grace looked confident as she came to bat. With a clenched jaw, she took two powerful warm-up swings and did her pre-pitch routine. Kayla's first pitch was a strike, and Grace smashed it right back at the pitcher. Kayla instinctively stuck her mitt up as she tumbled backward.

Thwack!

Somehow, the ball stuck in the webbing of her mitt for the third out. Grace, still holding her bat, raised her eyebrows and blinked in disbelief. That was the hardest ball she'd hit all season. The game remained tied, 2-2, with one inning to play.

Sophia took her warm-up pitches and then wiped the beads of sweat off her face with the back of her hand. She was throwing the best game of her life, against a very good hitting team.

"Let's go, Sophia. Have an inning. Get this first one," Zoe said as she bounced on the balls of her feet at shortstop.

Yeah, let's get this first one. Get her out, she thought as she glared in at Kayla, the Bandits' leadoff hitter.

The umpire signaled play ball, and Sophia wound up and sent the first pitch towards her catcher. Kayla swung, and the ball jumped off her bat. It was a line drive base hit between Emma at first and Addie at second. The Bandits had the go-ahead run on base.

"Get her if she tries to steal!" Coach Moore called, trying to be heard over the roar of the crowd.

Hannah, the Sting catcher, nodded to her coach.

Zoe put her hand to her mouth and called out to Addie, "She's fast, and they have a lefty up. I'll cover second."

Addie nodded in agreement.

"If she goes, let's get her, Hannah!" Zoe slapped her glove and took a step closer toward second base.

Violet Scott, the Bandits' tall first baseman, boldly marched to the plate. She batted from the left side of the plate and had a powerful swing. Earlier in the game, she clobbered one of Sophia's pitches for a long fly-out at the fence.

As the hitter stepped in, Zoe glanced at first base.

Kayla saw her looking, and a smirk came over her face. She energetically rocked on the base, ready to steal second.

"She's going! She's going!" Emma and Addie yelled in unison as Sophia's first pitch sped to the plate.

The ball was outside, and Violet didn't swing. Zoe scrambled to cover the base. Hannah snagged the pitch and fired towards second, but the throw sailed high. Zoe jumped and snagged the ball before awkwardly tumbling into short center field.

"Safe!" The umpire extended his arms as Kayla slid to a stop.

Zoe tossed the ball back to Sophia, rolled her shoulders, and trudged back to shortstop.

"Not quick enough to get me, huh? Now, watch me steal third," Kayla goaded, trying to get a reaction from Zoe.

Zoe felt her cheeks get hot but didn't give Kayla the satisfaction of a response. "You're okay, Sophia. Make your pitch." Zoe slammed her closed hand into her mitt and took a couple steps towards second base.

Sophia needed all the support she could get. The go-ahead run was on second base, and a very tough hitter stood at the plate. The Sting pitcher stepped to the back of the circle and took a few deep breaths before picking up some dirt and tossing it down.

"Play ball!" the umpire called as Violet stood impatiently in the batter's box.

Sophia got her sign from Hannah, reached into her glove, and grabbed the softball. She wound up and let her best fastball go. It made a beeline to the outside corner of home plate.

Kayla took off for third and had a great jump.

"Going! Going! Going!" every Sting player and fan seemed to scream.

Violet swung, and the softball cracked off her bat. It was a line drive up the middle, right at Zoe.

Smack!

In a split second, the ball was in Zoe's closed mitt. She instinctively stepped on second base. Double play! Two down!

The Sting's fans erupted in cheers as Coach Moore and the Sting bench clapped uncontrollably in the dugout. Sophia pumped her fist in the air and slapped her hand into her glove.

Addie grabbed Zoe's shoulder. "Wow, great play! I can't believe it!"

Both girls jumped up and down, broad smiles on their faces.

Kayla's mouth hung open as she stood near third base and looked back at Zoe and the Sting celebrating. The Bandits' third-base coach, still shaking her head, slowly waved Kayla off the field. As she reached the dugout, Kayla yanked her helmet off and tossed it on the ground. The Bandits' bench fell silent. Their fans uttered half-hearted words of encouragement from the stands.

Zoe shook the ball in her hand. "One more, one more! Get this next out, Sophia."

Sophia lifted her chin as she met Zoe near the back of the circle. A toothy grin came across her face as Zoe put the ball in her open glove.

"Yeah, let's get this out and go hit," the Sting pitcher said before turning toward home plate.

The Bandits' cleanup hitter, Elly Bowers, was next to bat. She was a dangerous hitter who led the Bandits in home runs the last two years. Elly stepped into the batter's box and smacked home plate with her bat. With her jaw clenched as she stared at Sophia.

Sophia, forehead scrunched, and eyes squinted, threw her best change-up. Elly's powerful swing was way too early. She swung so hard that she stumbled backward and nearly fell.

"Nice pitch!" Hannah exclaimed as she tossed the ball back to Sophia.

Let's throw her another change-up, Sophia thought as she slammed the softball into her glove, trying not to give away her plan.

The Sting pitcher wound up and let the slow pitch roll off her fingers. This time, Elly was ready and smashed it toward Abigail at third. The ball was hit so hard, it took one hop off of Abigail's shoulder and skipped right to Zoe. In one motion, Zoe scooped up the loose ball and fired a strike to Emma at first.

"Out!" barked the umpire as he forcefully lifted his right arm skyward.

It was a close play. So close that the Bandits' fans could be heard grumbling loudly in the first-base bleachers. A scowling Elly smacked the top of her helmet with both hands before shaking her head and slowly traipsing back to the dugout.

All the Sting players dashed off the field, except Abigail.

Abigail pulled up her left sleeve and saw a huge red mark on her arm. "Ouch!" Her lower lip quivered as she tried to lift her arm.

"Are you okay?" Coach Moore asked as she met Abigail halfway to the bench.

Trying to blink away the tears welling in her eyes, she said, "It really hurts. I'm supposed to bat first this inning, and I don't think I can swing a bat."

The coach put her arm around her and softly said, "Come in, sit down, and we'll get some ice on it."

The Sting players watched as the coach walked Abigail to the end of the bench.

"What's going on?" Kayla whispered between warm-up pitches. She tilted her head as she gazed at the commotion in the Sting dugout.

Coach Moore surveyed her players. "Ava, how are you feeling? Do you think you can bat?"

"Yeah! I'm feeling better. I can hit," she answered.

The coach pointed. "You're going to re-enter for Abigail and lead off the inning."

"Great! I'll get my helmet!" Ava hurriedly dodged her teammates as she headed to her bat bag.

"Let's go, Ava! Get it started." Addie slapped the team's star on her back as she quickly passed.

After throwing her last warm-up pitch, Kayla caught sight of Ava walking into the on-deck circle. Kayla's eyes widened, and her eyebrows raised. Her heart started to race, and butterflies flitted around in her stomach. She bit her lip and slowly rubbed the side of her face. This was not the hitter she wanted to face at this important point in the game.

The Sting bench and their fans cheered loudly as Ava confidently made her way to the batter's box. A quiet murmur filled the Bandits' side of the stands. Zoe noticed the Bandit outfielders taking several steps back.

Ava looked down at Coach Moore in the third-base coach's box as she lifted her white bat off her shoulder. Ava took a deep breath, studied her focal point, and then fixed her eyes outward towards the circle.

"C'mon, Ava! You can do it!" the coach yelled as she enthusiastically clapped.

Kayla looked in toward home plate, her gaze darting between her catcher and Ava. Kayla noticed her muscles tightening with each glance. Her chest heaved, but she still couldn't seem to get enough air.

Don't walk her. Don't walk her, Kayla repeated to herself while wiping her sweaty palm on the side of her jersey.

Zoe leaned closer to Addie. "Kayla looks nervous, and she's not taking a deep breath."

"Yeah, she should've been paying attention at the clinic," Addie said, shaking her head.

"Play ball," the umpire said, pointing to the pitcher.

Ava watched the first pitch sail way outside. The second pitch was inside and skipped in the dirt, nearly hitting her.

Hit the ball hard. Right up the middle. Rip it, Ava said to herself between pitches before doing her pre-pitch routine to turn off her thinking.

"Ava! You got this!" Zoe screamed as loud as she could to ensure Ava could hear her over the deafening crowd.

"This is who we want up right now. I think she's going to do it," Addie predicted without looking away from the field.

Kayla's mind was filled with racing thoughts. *What's wrong with me? I can't throw a strike. I'm terrible. I need to just get this one over somehow.* She reached into her glove and grabbed the softball for the next pitch.

She took speed off her fastball, trying to make sure she threw a strike. The ball sailed right down the middle ... and Ava took a powerful swing.

Smack!

The yellow softball jumped off the bat like it was shot out of a cannon and screamed skyward toward left field. Every person in the stands jumped to their feet. Players from both teams rushed to the front of their dugouts, trying to get a better look at the towering fly ball. Time seemed to slow down, maybe even stop.

It's gonna go out, Ava thought as she caught a glimpse of the ball while running down to first base.

"Go, ball. Go!" shouted Zoe, frantically hopping up and down.

Her back to the infield, the Bandits' left fielder sprinted as fast as she could, trying to catch up to the soaring softball. She came to a sudden halt and stared at the fence in front of her. The softball kept flying and escaped the park.

Homerun! The Sting won 3-2!

The Sting players ran out of the dugout like it was the last day of school and headed for home plate. Ava could do nothing but smile as she slapped Coach Moore's hand and watched her cheering teammates.

The celebration continued as Ava crossed home plate and felt her teammates press around her all the way to the dugout.

We are tournament champions! We finally beat the Bandits! Zoe thought as she followed Ava.

As the teams lined up and shook hands, the Sting players beamed with pride. There were no funny faces this time from the Bandits.

As each player on the Sting got their ring, the crowd cheered, and the team celebrated with high-fives and hugs.

Zoe held her ring up in the sun, admiring the sparkle. "Take a look at this ring! We're champions! I've never actually won a tournament before!"

"Everyone, let's get our picture at home plate!" Ava enthusiastically waved to the group.

"Let's go!" Addie squealed as she ran toward the backstop, and the other Sting players rushed to join her, still bouncing.

After the ring presentations, Coach Green asked to meet with the Sting in the outfield. Her college players, Emily, and Macy joined the group.

"Congratulations on a great game and tournament! I could tell that you used what you learned yesterday at the clinic," the coach said as she smiled at the group.

Emily pumped her fist. "That's how you play Arrows-Out. Despite falling behind and having

players get hurt, you kept competing as hard as you could."

"Keep using the positive self-talk, too," Macy added before high fiving Sophia, who stood nearby.

Coach Green ended by saying, "Congratulations, again, and best of luck the rest of the season."

"Bring it in here," Zoe said as she waved the girls into a huddle. "Go, Sting, on three!"

"One-two-three! Go, Sting!" the group shouted.

The girls couldn't stop grinning as they posed for more pictures, their arms draped around each other. The Sting players lingered by the dugout, savoring every last moment of their victory.

Zoe and Ava were among the last to leave.

"Great game, Ava. What a home run!" Zoe said as she slung her bat bag onto her back.

"Thanks, you played great, too," Ava said as the girls walked through the gate towards the parking lot.

"Listen!" exclaimed Ava with a huge smile.

Both girls stopped walking and looked to the right. Two young girls, who were maybe six years old, carrying softball mitts, were chanting,

"We don't mope! We don't pout! We just play Arrows-Out!"

Zoe and Ava looked at each other, nodding in approval. "Looks like we have some new Sting fans," Zoe said with a grin. They fist bumped each other, feeling like celebrities. Proud of their impact on the younger players, Zoe and Ava were excited for what the future held for the Sting.

Hit a Home Run – Answer These Questions

Chapter 2

1. Ava and Zoe talked about the Three Ts of the reset. What exactly are these steps? Write them on a piece of paper and keep it as a reminder of what you need to do. Pretend you just made a mistake and do those steps now.

2. "Tell Yourself Something Positive" is the last T. Coach Moore had the girls write down some positive things they'd say after making a mistake. Make a list of three things you'll tell yourself after an error and three things you'll tell yourself after a bad at-bat.

3. Coach Moore and Ava demonstrated the four steps of a good pre-pitch routine to the team. List the four steps.

4. When Ava showed her focal point to the team, she and Coach Moore said it should be something small. She said you should study it closely. What does studying the focal point do for the hitter? Get your bat and decide on your focal point. Pretend you're coming to bat and go through your pre-pitch routine.

Chapter 3

1. Zoe was nervous when she and Ava arrived at the college softball clinic. Ava told her a good way to relax in any situation is to take deep breaths. Besides softball games, when could you use this type of deep breathing to help you feel less anxious? Take a few deep breaths right now. Don't forget to do them correctly by smelling the roses and blowing out birthday candles.

2. Kayla was missing ground balls and was also getting frustrated in the batting cage. What would you tell her if you were her coach?

Chapter 4

1. Coach Green wrote "Win the Next Pitch" on the board and said this should be a player's main goal. What exactly did she mean by that? What skills help players get ready to win the next pitch?

2. What does it mean to play "Arrows-In?" What does it mean to play "Arrows-Out?" The college players told the girls that when they made mistakes, they automatically felt an Arrows-In attitude but had taught themselves to quickly switch it to an Arrows-Out attitude. Ava and Zoe made up a chant to help them remember to switch from Arrows-In to Arrows Out. Write the chant down.

Chapter 5

1. Emily and Macy also taught the Sting players about the importance of having positive self-talk. What are the Four Ss of self-talk?

2. "Shred the Arrows-In Words" was one of the Ss. What are some Arrows-In words that need shredding? Imagine that you were telling yourself some of these things during a game. Now, picture a huge shredder gobbling up those negative words. If you start saying Arrows-In words when you are playing, use your shredder!

3. Macy also said to always "Say *what you want to have happen*, instead of what you're *afraid* might happen." What did she mean by this? Can you give some examples? Pretend you are on-deck or walking

up to bat. What will you say to yourself instead of "Don't strike out?"

Chapter 6

1. In her first at-bat against the Wolves, Addie said she forgot to use her mental game skills. What did she change that helped her the next time up to bat?

2. Reread Zoe's last at-bat against the Wolves. What did she do well?

3. Pretend you were in Zoe's position, coming up to bat. Practice your positive self-talk and do your pre-pitch routine.

Chapter 7

1. Find examples in this chapter of Sting players who did a reset.

2. After Ava got hurt, what did she remind the team to do?

3. Make a list of at least five things you learned from reading this book.

Strategies for Coaches and Parents

One of the most important things you can do to help a young player learn these skills is to make sure they practice them regularly so they are automatic during games. Young players often need to be reminded to reset, use their pre-pitch routines, and have an Arrows-Out attitude. Consistent encouragement is the key. Below are some ways to help players learn, remember, and master the skills.

This age group loves to be creative! After the girls have finished reading the book, have them get together and create mental game reminders about what they've learned. A great way to do this is to use markers, glitter, construction paper, and paint to create reminder posters (a sheet of copy paper is fine). Coaches can laminate the posters and different players' posters can be hung in the dugout at each game or tournament. This is a fun way to create visual reminders for game day.

Reminder posters might include:

Win the Next Pitch.

Play Arrows-Out

The Arrows-Out Chant

The Three Ts

The Steps in the Pre-Pitch Routine

The Four Ss of Self-Talk

Another fun activity that can be done is to get luggage tags at a dollar store and have each player create a mental game reminder for themselves. They can then attach the reminder tag to their bat bag so it's there during games. Players can make more than one message and switch them out as the season goes along.

When practicing the pre-pitch routine, do not rush it. Most players will want to take a quick glance at the focal point and then try to hit. In my clinics, I have found a method of introducing the focal point that works very well —

Use front toss, with each player getting 3-5 swings at a time before rotating. It is good to do this in groups of 3 or 4, as the girls will learn a lot by watching their teammates. Have each girl show you what focal point they will use. Here, you can make sure it is small and as unique as possible.

Tell the hitters that you're just practicing on the focal point and not to worry about mechanics or how hard they hit the ball. (The key goal for this drill is to get them to experience hitting without thinking.)

Instruct them to take their time and look at their focal point as long as it takes until they aren't thinking, and then the eyes go to the release point. It may take five seconds or even longer, which is okay. The key is not to rush it. A simple glance does not help us get the external, narrow focus we want.

Teach players to practice positive self-talk when they are in-the-hole and on-deck. This is particularly important when they're facing a very tough pitcher. Young players often think about their fear of striking out or getting hit by the ball (things they do not want to have happen). In practice, have them practice, saying what they want to have happen instead - 'hit the ball hard,' instead. Be sure to remind them during the game to do this.

I always like it when the team has the batter who is in-the-hole track down the hitter's bat instead of the batter who is coming to the plate. The on-deck batter has just spent time getting focused and ready to hit, and I don't want her to be distracted by having to track down the bat. It's a simple thing, but it makes a difference.

Finally, don't forget to stress that softball can be a tough game, and no one plays perfectly. The goal is to play hard, learn as much as possible, and have fun. Perfectionism at this early age will make playing a negative experience and can lead to burnout.

Acknowledgements

I'd like to thank the many coaches and players I've worked with over the years. Together, we've exchanged constructive, positive, and usable techniques, leading to much success. And, of course, we had a lot of fun along the way!

I'd like to thank those who provided support and suggestions throughout the writing process. Nicole Smith, thank you for being my advisor for all things softball. Olivia Fisher, thanks again, for being my editor for book two. You continue to teach me so much about writing and your skillful editing made this book so much better.

Last but not least, I'd like to thank my wife, Dianne, for her support, patience, and wise suggestions throughout the writing process.

About the Author

Dr. Curt Ickes is a licensed clinical psychologist who also specializes in sport psychology and has an undying love for baseball and softball. He is fascinated by the application of psychology in sports and teaches techniques that lead to optimal athletic performance. Having taught psychology at Ashland University in Ohio for over three decades (go Eagles!), Dr. Ickes is a professor emeritus at the university and continues his involvement with the AU baseball team. In addition to the Eagles, he works with many other baseball and softball teams. He was also the sport psychologist for the Lake Erie Crushers, a professional baseball team. Curt's first published book, *Mental Toughness: Getting the Edge,* covers sport psychology and mental game skills for more advanced baseball players. His best-selling books, *You Got This!* and *Win the Next Pitch!* introduce young softball and baseball players to important mental game skills that build confidence and immediately improve game performance. These books are available on Amazon.com.

Curt hopes his book helps aspiring softball players enjoy the sport even more by teaching them mental game skills and concepts to help them succeed on the field. He also believes that younger athletes can apply these skills in other sports and performance settings. Developing a tough mentality makes children feel more positive about themselves and their teammates. It also helps them understand how best to cope with the inevitable emotions that surround triumph and failure.

The Arrows-Out Chant!

We don't mope!
We don't pout!
We just play !
ARROWS-OUT!

Made in the USA
Middletown, DE
13 August 2024